普通高等学校城市轨道交通专业规划教材组织委员会

主　任　　罗　斌　　王丰胜
副主任　　储继红　　胡勇健　　刘明亮　　李　锐
委　员　　郑　斌　　廉　星　　刘蓉蓉　　朱海燕　　李建洋　　娄　智
　　　　　　杨光明　　左美生

普通高等学校城市轨道交通专业规划教材编写委员会

主　编　　李　锐　　刘蓉蓉
副主编　　郑　斌　　段明华
编　委　　张国侯　　李宇辉　　穆中华　　左美生　　娄　智　　李志成
　　　　　　兰清群　　钟晓旭　　李队员　　王晓飞　　李泽军　　李艳艳
　　　　　　颜　争　　彭　骏　　黄建中　　周云娣　　陈　谦　　黄远春
　　　　　　田　亮　　文　杰　　任志杰　　李国伟　　薛　亮　　牛云霞
　　　　　　张　荣　　苏　颖　　孔　华　　高剑锋　　储　粲　　孙醒鸣
　　　　　　罗　涛　　胡永军　　洪　飞　　韦允城　　吴文苗　　钟　高
　　　　　　张诗航　　张敬文　　武止戈　　吴　柳　　赵　猛　　沙　磊
　　　　　　吴　仃　　赵瑞雪　　聂化东　　彭元龙　　胡　啸　　干　慧
　　　　　　项红叶　　马晓丹　　孙　欣　　邹正军　　余泳逸

普通高等学校"十三五"省级规划教材
普通高等学校城市轨道交通专业规划教材

城市轨道交通专业英语

Professional English for Urban Rail Transit

主　编　李艳艳　兰清群
副主编　邓春兰　彭　骏
编写人员（以姓氏笔画为序）
　　　　王莹莹　王艳锦　邓春兰
　　　　兰清群　吴红云　李艳艳
　　　　徐婷婷　彭　骏
主　审　李　锐

中国科学技术大学出版社

内容简介

本书包含城市轨道交通系统分类、信号系统、运营管理、车辆构造、机电系统、供电系统、通信系统、单轨系统、全自动运行系统等9章内容,每章由课文、术语、练习等模块组成。本书在编写过程中充分考虑学术英语的应用场景设计,结合学生发展的阶段性需求,有针对性地帮助学生掌握专业英语的相关知识。同时,增加开放性课题讨论环节,引导学生搜集相关专业的学术和行业资料,以此训练学生资料搜集和英语阅读的能力。

图书在版编目(CIP)数据

城市轨道交通专业英语/李艳艳,兰清群主编. —合肥:中国科学技术大学出版社,2022.7
(普通高等学校城市轨道交通专业规划教材)
ISBN 978-7-312-05456-3

Ⅰ. 城… Ⅱ. ①李… ②兰… Ⅲ. 城市铁路—轨道交通—英语 Ⅳ. U239.5

中国版本图书馆 CIP 数据核字(2022)第100638号

城市轨道交通专业英语
CHENGSHI GUIDAO JIAOTONG ZHUANYE YINGYU

出版	中国科学技术大学出版社
	安徽省合肥市金寨路96号,230026
	http://press.ustc.edu.cn
	https://zgkxjsdxcbs.tmall.com
印刷	安徽省瑞隆印务有限公司
发行	中国科学技术大学出版社
开本	787 mm×1092 mm 1/16
印张	12.25
字数	374千
版次	2022年7月第1版
印次	2022年7月第1次印刷
定价	42.00元

Foreword 序

本套教材根据城市轨道交通运营管理、城市轨道交通通信信号技术、城市轨道交通车辆技术、城市轨道交通机电技术、城市轨道交通供配电技术专业的人才培养需要，结合对职业岗位能力的要求，由安徽交通职业技术学院、南京铁道职业技术学院、郑州铁路职业技术学院、上海工程技术大学、沈阳交通高等专科学校、新疆交通职业技术学院、合肥职业技术学院、合肥铁路工程学校、合肥市轨道交通集团有限公司、深圳城市轨道交通运营公司、杭州城市轨道交通运营公司、宁波城市轨道交通运营公司、郑州铁路局等单位共同编写。

本套教材整合了国内主要城市轨道交通运营企业现场作业的内容，以实际工作项目为主线，以项目中的具体工作任务作为知识学习要点，并针对各项任务设计模拟实训与思考练习，实现了通过课堂环境模拟现场岗位作业情景促进学生自我学习、自我训练的目标，体现了"岗位导向、学练一体"的教学理念。

本套教材涵盖城市轨道交通运营管理、城市轨道交通通信信号技术、城市轨道交通车辆技术、城市轨道交通机电技术、城市轨道交通供配电技术专业，可作为以上各相关专业课程的教材，并可供相关城市轨道交通运营企业相关人员参考。

普通高等学校城市轨道交通专业规划教材编写委员会

Preface
前言

截至 2020 年底,中国内地累计有 40 个城市开通城市轨道交通。随着城市化进程的进一步加速,中国的城市轨道交通建设有望迎来黄金发展期,本书在此背景下编写而成,以反映轨道交通行业前沿成果。目前,我国轨道交通专业英语教材普遍存在内容广而不精、深度不够的问题,主要表现在大部分高职院校所用教材立足于轨道交通企业运营管理岗位的实际工作,内容上侧重与实操作业相关的英文术语,而缺乏理论和概念层面的介绍。本书在编写过程中明确专业英语的切入点,注重学思结合、知行统一,尤其是在选材上特别注重所选材料的标准性、相关性和代表性,为学生的专业技术能力和基础学术能力的培养奠定基础。

本书共有 9 章,每章由课文、术语、练习等模块组成,对城市轨道交通系统分类、信号系统、运营管理、车辆构造、机电系统、供电系统、通信系统、单轨系统、全自动运行系统等方面进行了详细介绍,满足轨道交通不同专业的教学需求,教师在教学时可以灵活选择教学篇章。同时,书中设置了英语写作部分,从实用的角度出发,帮助学生提高英语写作能力,提升综合素养。本书体例新颖,结构合理,专业知识面广,各章节附有英文视频资料,供学生观看学习(可联系 958972212@qq.com 索取)。

本书所选的参考材料源于国内外轨道交通专业书籍和资料、城市轨道交通网站、相关专业文献、事故调查报告、轨道交通相关行业标准等,保证了教材的广度、深度和针对性,同时确保了内容的真实性和表达方式的原汁原味。本书针对高职学生的英语实际水平,在词汇、句型等方面适当降低难度,注重语言的实际运用和专业知识的积累。

本书由安徽交通职业技术学院李艳艳、兰清群担任主编,邓春兰、彭骏担任副主编,李锐担任主审,李艳艳负责统筹整理全书。具体编写分工如下:兰清群编写第 1 章、第 4 章的主体部分,王艳锦编写第 2 章的主体部分,李艳艳编写第 3 章、第 9 章的主体部分,彭骏编写第 5 章的主体部分,邓春兰编写第 6 章、第 8 章的主体部分,徐婷婷编写第 7 章的主体部分；第1至第7章中的写作部分由吴红云、王莹莹编写，第8章、第9章中的写作部分由李艳艳编写。

由于本书涵盖内容广泛，加之编写时间有限、编者业务水平有限，书中难免会有疏漏和不足之处，恳请广大读者给予批评指正。

编　者

2022年2月

Contents
目录

Foreword ·· (i)

Preface ·· (iii)

Chapter 1 Introduction to Urban Rail Transit ··································· (1)
    1.1 Urban Transport Modes ·· (5)
    1.2 Prospect of Rail Transit ·· (5)
    1.3 Writing: Email Basics ·· (7)
    1.4 KEY TERMS ·· (13)
    1.5 EXERCISES ·· (14)

Chapter 2 Signal System ··· (16)
    2.1 Signal Basic Equipment ·· (16)
    2.2 Block System ·· (21)
    2.3 Interlock System ·· (26)
    2.4 Automatic Train Control System ·· (32)
    2.5 Communication Based Train Control System ·· (42)
    2.6 KEY TERMS ·· (46)
    2.7 EXERCISES ·· (47)

Chapter 3 Operation & Management ·· (49)
    3.1 Station Operation ·· (49)
    3.2 Train Operation ·· (63)

3.3	Safe Operations Requirements	(68)
3.4	Emergency Management	(72)
3.5	Writing: How to Write Job Applications	(79)
3.6	KEY TERMS	(81)
3.7	EXERCISES	(83)

Chapter 4 Subway Train (85)

4.1	Car Body	(85)
4.2	Bogie	(87)
4.3	Brake System	(90)
4.4	Couplers	(91)
4.5	Traction System	(93)
4.6	Train Operation	(94)
4.7	KEY TERMS	(97)
4.8	EXERCISES	(99)

Chapter 5 Electromechanical Equipment (100)

5.1	Platform Screen Door	(100)
5.2	Lift	(104)
5.3	Escalator	(108)
5.4	Automatic Fare Collection System	(110)
5.5	Integrated Supervision and Control System	(113)
5.6	Ventilation and Air Conditioning System	(115)
5.7	Writing: How to Write Invitation	(116)
5.8	KEY TERMS	(118)
5.9	EXERCISES	(119)

Chapter 6 Power and Catenary (121)

6.1	Power Supply	(121)
6.2	Overhead Line (Catenary)	(125)
6.3	Power Supply Safety	(131)
6.4	Writing: How to Write An Email Requesting Something	(137)
6.5	KEY TERMS	(141)
6.6	EXERCISES	(142)

Chapter 7 Telcom System (144)

7.1	Structure of Telcom System	(144)

7.2　Function of Subsystem ………………………………………………… (145)
7.3　Writing: Introduction to Notice ……………………………………… (155)
7.4　KEY TERMS ……………………………………………………………… (156)
7.5　EXERCISES ……………………………………………………………… (157)

Chapter 8　Monorail ……………………………………………………… (158)
8.1　Types of Monorail ……………………………………………………… (158)
8.2　Overview of Chongqing Monorail …………………………………… (161)
8.3　Writing: How to Write A Summary …………………………………… (166)
8.4　KEY TERMS ……………………………………………………………… (167)
8.5　EXERCISES ……………………………………………………………… (167)

Chapter 9　Fully Automatic Operation (FAO) ………………………… (169)
9.1　Grades of Fully Automatic Operation ……………………………… (170)
9.2　Autonomous Train Applications ……………………………………… (172)
9.3　Challenges from the Deployment of ATs …………………………… (174)
9.4　Writing: How to Write A Report ……………………………………… (178)
9.5　KEY TERMS ……………………………………………………………… (180)
9.6　EXERCISES ……………………………………………………………… (180)

References …………………………………………………………………… (182)

Chapter 1 Introduction to Urban Rail Transit

> Urban rail transit is an all-encompassing term for various types of local rail systems providing passenger service within and around urban or suburban areas. The set of urban rail systems can be roughly subdivided into the following categories, which sometimes overlap because some systems or lines have aspects of multiple types: tram, light rail, rapid transit, commuter rail, AGT etc.

1.1 Urban Transport Modes

1.1.1 Tram

A tram, streetcar, or trolley system is a rail-based transit system that runs mainly or completely along streets (i.e. with street running), with a relatively low capacity and frequent stops. Passengers usually board at street-level or curb-level, although low-floor trams may allow level boarding. Longer-distance lines are called interurbans or radial railways. Few interurbans remain, most having been upgraded to commuter rail or light rail, or else abandoned.

The term "tram" is used in most parts of the world. Hong Kong Tramways in China is shown in figure 1.1. In North America, these systems are referred as "streetcar" or "trolley" systems; in Germany, such systems are called "street train" or "street railway". Updated tram systems have higher passenger capacities than traditional streetcars.

1.1.2 Light Rail

A light rail system is a rail-based transit system that has higher capacity and speed than a tram, usually by operating in an exclusive right-of-way separated from automobile traffic, but which is not (as rapid transit is) fully grade-separated from other traffic.

Light rail also generally operates with multiple units trains rather than single tramcars. It emerged as an evolution of trams/streetcars. Light rail systems vary significantly in terms of speed and capacity. They range from slightly improved tram systems to systems that are essentially rapid transit but with some level crossings.

Figure 1.1 Hong Kong tramways

The term "light rail" is the most common term used, though German systems are called to "city railway". Sydney light rail is shown in figure 1.2.

Figure 1.2 Sydney light rail

1.1.3 Rapid Transit (Metro or Subway)

A rapid transit system is a railway — usually in an urban area — with high passenger capacities and frequency of service, and (usually) full grade separation from other traffic (including other rail traffic). It is often known as "heavy rail" to distinguish it from light rail and bus rapid transit.

In most parts of the world, these systems are known as a "metro" which is short for "metropolitan". The term "subway" is used in many American systems, as well as in Glasgow and Toronto. The system in London is named the "underground" and commonly nicknamed the "tube". Systems in Germany are called the underground track. Many systems in East, Southeast and South Asia are called "MRT" which stands for "mass rapid transit". Systems which are predominantly elevated may be referred to as "L" as in Chicago or "SkyTrain", as in Bangkok and Vancouver. Paris Metro is shown in figure 1.3.

Figure 1.3 Paris Metro

1.1.4 Monorail

A monorail is a railway in which the track consists of a single rail, as opposed to the traditional track with two parallel rails. A monorail is a railway in which the track consists of a single rail or a beam. The term is also used to describe the beam of the system, or the trains traveling on such a beam or track. The term originates from joining "mono" (meaning one) and "rail" from 1897, possibly from German engineer Eugen Langen, who called an elevated railway system with wagons suspended the Eugen Langen One-railed Suspension Tramway. German H-Bahn Monorail is shown in figure 1.4.

1.1.5 Commuter Rail

A commuter rail, regional rail, or suburban rail system operates on mainline trackage which may be shared with intercity rail and freight trains. Systems tend to operate at lower frequencies than rapid transit or light rail systems but tend to travel at higher speeds, have more widely spaced stations, and cover longer overall distances. They have high passenger capacities per single train.

Figure 1.4 German H-Bahn monorail

Though many European and East Asian commuter rail systems operate with frequencies and rolling stock similar to that of rapid transit, they do not qualify as such because they share tracks with intercity/freight trains or have at grade crossings. For example, S-trains are hybrid systems combining the characteristics of rapid transit and commuter rail systems. Generally, S-trains share tracks with mainline passenger and freight trains, but distances between stations and service headway resemble Metro systems.

Transit agencies' names for lines do not necessarily reflect their technical. For example, Boston's Green Line is referred to as a subway, despite being mostly made up of above-ground portions. Conversely, the Docklands Light Railway in London, Green Line in Los Angeles, and some metro lines in China are referred to as "Light Rail" even though they qualify as rapid transit because they are fully grade-separated and provide a high frequency of service.

Many cities use names such as subway and elevated railway to describe their entire systems, even when they combine both methods of operation. Slightly less than half of the London Underground's tracks, for example, are actually underground; New York City's subway also combines elevated and subterranean stations, while the Chicago "L" and Vancouver SkyTrain use tunnels to run through central areas.

A bus shares many characteristics with light rail and trams but does not run on rails. Trolley buses are buses that are powered from overhead wires. Vehicles that can travel both on rails and on roads have been tried experimentally, but are not in common use. The term bus rapid transit is used to refer to various methods of providing faster bus services and the systems which use it have similar characteristics to light rail. Some cities experimenting with guided bus technologies, such as Nancy, have chosen to refer to them as "trams on tires" (rubber-tired trams) and given them tram-like appearances. Manchester Commuter rail is shown in figure 1.5.

Figure 1.5 Manchester Commuter rail

Public rail transit provides certain benefits for a community, but also that the goals of policymakers are not often met. They also say some American economists claim that, contrary to popular belief, rail transit has failed to improve the environment, serve the poor, or reduce highway congestion in the United States. They also say economists are somewhat more optimistic about rail transit's impact on economic development.

1.2 Prospect of Rail Transit

Metro systems have been constructed very intensively in many countries around the world since the 1950s, increasing the number of cities with metros from 17 to 110. A large share of RRT (Rail Rapid Transit) construction during the 1950～1980 period (nearly 40%) took place in western Europe, Japan, and North America. Tokyo, Seoul, Madrid and a number of other cities have drastically increased their metro networks and introduced many technical and operational innovations in recent decades. However, an increasing share of construction has subsequently been done in the newly urbanizing countries (Brazil, Egypt, India, China).

Several comprehensive studies of interactions between rail transit and urban characteristics have a major significance for estimating the future development of rail transit. Namely, cities with rail and bus transit compared with those served by buses only have:

- Significantly higher transit riding habit (annual transit trips per capita).
- Considerably lower auto travel per capita.

- Distinctly lower total energy consumption per capita.

Although many other factors have influences on these statistical findings, there is little doubt that rail transit, through its characteristics, has a strong influence on transit use and the form of cities in the long run. Consequently, the future development of rail transit is closely related to the trend of growth and future characteristics of cities. If transportation policies and planning efforts are concentrated on serving growing cities and their economic vitality, expansion of rail transit should represent a major component of those efforts. Rail rapid transit has been continuously expanded and innovated with new concepts in many cities.

As in Europe and North America, an increasing diversification of rail modes has occurred worldwide. As in the United States, cities in many other countries have upgraded existing or built entirely new light rail systems. Their central city sections have been built in many cities in tunnels or in pedestrian zones, and sub-urban sections have been built in about 30 German cities, 15 French, and 5 British cities. Other cities building new LRT have been those in Spain, The Netherlands, Switzerland, Ireland, Turkey, and many eastern European countries.

Major regional rail modernizations, and construction of entirely new lines, have also been undertaken in numerous countries. Particularly interesting deve-lopments are found in Paris (R. E. R.), Berlin, Munich, Frankfurtand Ruhr (S-Bahn), several Brazilian, and many Japanese cities. There is a strong trend in many countries to introduce bilevel cars for increased seating capacity. The recently developed tram-train concept, unifying the light rail and regional rail modes, is likely to be introduced in more urban regions in the future.

With respect to the dominant reasons for metro construction, cities around the world can be classified into two rather distinct categories. Cities in western Europe, the United States, and Canada build rail transit systems primarily to improve the quality of their transit services, to make them capable of attracting passengers from the automobile. Cities in Latin America, Asia, and to a large extent Russia and other members of the former USSR build metro systems primarily to provide the needed high capacity, i.e., quantity of service (improved service is, of course, always another important contributing factor).

The importance of both of these dominant requirements — quality and quantity of service — has increased in recent years. High auto ownership has resulted in the paralysis of cities; urbanization, particularly intensive in the developing countries, has created growing needs for higher-capacity systems than highway modes can provide. The result of these trends has been continuously accelerating construction of metro systems throughout the world, as discussed above.

In addition to the need for increased capacity and improved quality of transit services, several other aspects of metros (or rail transit in general) have an important role in the decisions about their construction. Introduction of a metro is always an important step in the development of a city. Its construction usually represents the largest and most significant public project ever undertaken by the city; it stimulates various planning activities and interest in civic progress in general. Its opening is always a major festivity: inaugurations of the metro and other major rail systems in Brussels, London, Paris, and Vienna were made in presence of heads of the respective countries.

The opening of rail transit lines results in a major reduction in energy consumption for transportation as well as for other purposes. These savings increase with time through the impact of rail transit on urban forms. Moreover, the rail transit system becomes a landmark by itself, giving the city a certain special identity and image. There is a distinct pride in a city's being a "metro city". Most great world cities are recognized as such partly because of their metro systems: an important part of Paris is the Metro; of London, the Underground; of New York, the Subway; of Moscow, the Metropolitan; and of Berlin, the U-Bahn. Light rail is similarly a symbol of livable, pedestrian, and transit-oriented cities in San Francisco, Portland, Calgary, Cologne, Karlsruhe, and many other cities. The importance and value of rail transit thus considerably exceeds the direct physical and economic results of its operations. Regional rail usually represents a distinct symbol of a large region with its central city strongly connected with its surrounding areas. In addition to very large metropolitan areas such as Tokyo, London, and New York, good examples of this role of regional rail are Munich, Sydney, and Los Angeles as a new member of this category of urbanized regions.

1.3 Writing: Email Basics

Introduction to Email

Do you ever feel like the only person who doesn't use email? You don't have to feel left out. If you're just getting started, you'll see that with a little bit of practice, email is easy to understand and use.

In this section, you will learn what email is, how it compares to traditional mail, and how email addresses are written. We'll also discuss various types of email providers and the features and tools they include with an email account.

Getting to Know Email

Electronic mail (Email) is a way to send and receive messages across the Internet.

Email is shown in figure 1.6. It's similar to traditional mail, but it also has some key differences. Traditional mail is shown in figure 1.7. To get a better idea of what email is all about, take a look at the table 1.1 and consider how you might benefit from its use.

Figure 1.6　Email

Figure 1.7　Traditional mail

Table 1.1　Traditional Mail vs Email

Compare Items	Traditional Mail	Email
Address	Traditional mail is addressed with the recipient's name, street address, city, state or province, and zip code. For example, it will usually look something like this: Taihu road 22, Hefei city, Anhui province of China, 230051.	Email address are always written in a standard format, but they look quite different from traditional mail. An email address includes: a username, the @ (at) symbol, and the email provider's domain. Usernames often include numbers and shortened versions of a name to create unique email address, and will usually look something like this: admin55@qq.com.
Delivery	Traditional mail in a sealed envelope or package is delivered to a home or post office box by a mail carrier.	Email is delivered electronically across the Internet. It is received by the inbox of an email service provider like QQ, Yahoo, or 163.
Time	Traditional mail delivery could take anywhere between a couple of days, to a couple of weeks, depending on where it's being sent.	Email is deliverd instantly, or usually within a few minutes.

Advantages of Email

Productivity tools: Email is usually packaged with a calendar, address book, instant messaging, and more for convenience and productivity.

- **Access to web services**: If you want to sign up for an account like Oracle or order products from services like Amazon, you will need an **email address** so you can be safely identified and contacted.
- **Easy mail management**: Email service providers have tools that allow you to file, label, prioritize, find, group, and filter your emails for easy **management**. You can even easily control **spam**, or **junk email**.
- **Privacy**: Your email is delivered to your own personal and private account with a **password** required to **access** and **view** emails.
- **Communication with multiple people**: You can send an email to multiple people at once, giving you the option to include as few as or as many people as you want in a conversation.
- **Accessible anywhere at any time**: You don't have to be at home to get your mail. You can access it from any computer or mobile device that has an Internet connection.

Understanding Email Addresses

To receive emails, you will need an email account and an email address. Also, if you want to send emails to other people, you will need to obtain their email addresses. It's important to learn how to write email addresses correctly because if you do not enter them exactly right, your emails will not be delivered or might be delivered to the wrong person.

Email addresses are always written in a standard format that includes a user name, the @ (at) symbol, and the email provider's domain. Email address — username is shown in figure 1.8.

Designing an Effective SQL Data Lakehouse ☆
From: KDnuggets <editor1@kdnuggets.com>
    (Send by behalf of bounce-mc.us12_50554633.323097-0fc8927298@mail117.atl111.rsgsv.net)
Date: Monday, Jan 31, 2022 5:19 PM
To: hywei <hyweisky@foxmail.com>

Figure 1.8 Email address — username

The user name is the name you choose to identify yourself.

The email provider is the website that hosts your email account.

Some businesses and organizations use email addresses with their own website domain. Email address — provider is shown in figure 1.9. Customized email address is shown in figure 1.10.

Figure 1.9 Email address — provider

Figure 1.10 Customized email address

About Email Providers

In the past, people usually received an email account from the same companies that provided their Internet access. For example, if QQ provided your Internet connection, you'd have an QQ email address. While this is still true for some people, today it's increasingly common to use a free web-based email ser-vice, also known as Webmail. Anyone can use these services, no matter who provides their Internet access.

Webmail Providers

Today, the top two webmail providers are QQ and Net Ease(mail.163). These providers are popular because they allow you to access your email account from anywhere with an Internet connection. You can also access webmail on your mobile device. Top 2 webmails of China are shown in figure 1.11.

Figure 1.11 Top 2 webmails of China

Other Email Providers

Many people also have an email address hosted by their company, school, or organization. These email addresses are usually for professional purposes. For example, the people who work for this website have email addresses that end with @163.com. If you are part of an organization that hosts your email, they'll show you how to access it.

Many hosted web domains end with a suffix other than .com. Depending on the organization, your provider's domain might end with a suffix like. gov (for government websites),. edu (for schools), . mil (for military branches), or. org (for nonprofit organizations).

Email Applications

Many companies and organizations use an email application, like Microsoft Outlook, for communicating and managing their email. This software can be used with any email provider but is most commonly used by organizations that host their own email.

Email Productivity Features

In addition to email access, webmail providers offer various tools and features. These features are part of a productivity suite — a set of applications that help you work, communicate, and stay organized. The tools offered will vary by provider, but all major webmail services offer the following features:
- Instant messaging, or chat, which lets you have text-based conversations with other users.
- An online address book, where you can store contact information for the people you contact frequently. Address books is shown in figure 1. 12.

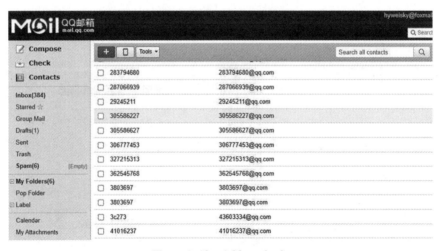

Figure 1. 12   Address books

- An online calendar to help organize your schedule and share it withothers. Online calendar of QQ-email is shown in figure 1. 13.

Getting Started with Email

You should now have a good understanding of what email is all about. Over the next few lessons, we will continue to cover essential email basics, etiquette, and safety tips.

Figure 1.13　Online calendar of QQ-email

Setting Up Your Own Email Account

If you want to sign up for your own email account, we suggest choosing from one of the two major webmail providers. But the simplest way is that as long as you have a QQ account, you have a QQ Email (figure 1.14).

- QQMail — http://mail.qq.com

- NetEase Mail — https://mail.163.com

Figure 1.14　QQMail and NetEase Mail

Practice Using An Email Program

Keep in mind that this tutorial will not show you how to use a specific email account. For that, you will need to visit QQ Email tutorial. It's a useful course for learning the basics, even if you ultimately end up choosing an email provider other than Gmail, such as Yahoo! or Outlook.com. There, you will learn how to:
- Sign up for an email account.
- Navigate and get to know the email interface.
- Compose, manage, and respond to email.
- Set up email on a mobile device.

Sample — Mail for Help

Dear Prof. Smith,

　　Could you please do me a favor at 10:00 am on Monday, August 29? I am on a business trip, and it will be delayed until next month, so I really need you to run the monthly seminar in our department for me.

　　I know it might take some preparation time, but you are the only one I can count on, and I know that you are more than qualified to run this event. Please let me know if you can help.

　　I look forward to hearing from you and I hope I can return the favor sometime.
Sincerely yours,
David

1.4　KEY TERMS

(1) urban rail transit
(2) passenger service
(3) tram
(4) light rail transit
(5) rapid transit
(6) commuter rail
(7) automatic guide transit (AGT)
(8) urban transport modes
(9) monorail
(10) commuter rail

(11) rubber-tired tram
(12) urbanized region
(13) rolling stock
(14) rubber-tired trams
(15) streetcar
(16) freight train

1.5 EXERCISES

I Match the terms with the correct definitions below.

| subwayrail transit   automatic guide transit (AGT)   light rail (LRT) |
| commuter rail   monorail |

1. All forms of non-highway ground transportation that run on rail. (   )

2. An underground rail rapid transit system or the tunnel through which it runs. (   )

3. A passenger railroad service that operates within metropolitan areas on trackage that usually is part of the general railroad system. The operations, primarily for commuters, are generally run as part of a regional system that is publicly owned or by a railroad company as part of its overall service. In some areas it is called regional rail.
(   )

4. Any guided transit mode with fully automated operation (i.e., no crew on the transit units). The term usually refers, however, only to guided modes with small and medium-sized vehicles that operate on guideways with exclusive right-of-way. (   )

5. A metropolitan electric railway system characterized by its ability to operate single cars or short trains along exclusive rights-of-way at ground level, on aerial structures, in subways, or occasionally, in streets, and to board and discharge passengers at track or car floor level. (   )

6. A transit system consisting of vehicles supported and guided by a single guideway (rail or beam), usually elevated. (   )

II **Answer the following questions according to the text.**

1. List and explain the characteristics of rail modes as well as distinguished from other transportation.

2. What are the differences between LRT and monorail?

3. Describe characteristics with respect to metro and monorail.

4. Discuss recent trends about urban rail transit.

Chapter 2 Signal System

> Railway signaling is a safety system used on railways to prevent trains from colliding. Trains are uniquely susceptible to collision because of running on fixed rails. They are not capable of avoiding a collision by steering away, and as can a road vehicle; furthermore, trains cannot decelerate rapidly, and are frequently operating at speeds where by the time the driver can see an obstacle, the train cannot stop in time to avoid colliding with it.
>
> Most forms of train control involve messages being passed from those in charge of the rail network or portions of it to the train crew, these are known as "signals" and from this the topic of train control is known as "signaling".
>
> The railway signaling equipments are mainly the signal, interlocking apparatus and block device. Instruction displayed by signal indications are for persons concerned in train running and shunting movement. Interlocking deals with the locking of routes, switches and signals at stations in proper arrangement. Block system is a mean to guide the train operation through a certain railway section.

2.1 Signal Basic Equipment

2.1.1 Track Circuit

The track circuit is a circuit made of the rail track and rail insulation. It is used to monitor the occupancy of the track and to link the train operation with signal displays, which is to transmit running information to the train through the track circuit. The track circuit is the important basic equipment of railway signal, and its performance directly affects the traffic safety and transportation efficiency.

The simplest form of track circuit is an insulated section of track with a relay on one end and with a battery, or some other source of energy on the other end. Figure 2.1 shows an elementary track circuit.

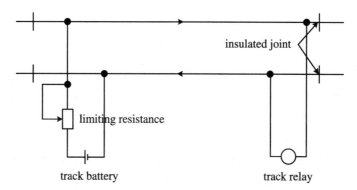

Figure 2.1 Simplified diagram of a track circuit

It consists of the following:

A source of energy — for example, a battery.

A limiting resistance, so called because it limits the current from the battery.

Rails and rail bonding, both offering resistance.

Ties and ballast, both offering a path for current leakage from rail. This path has resistance, referred to as "ballast resistance".

Relay series resistance (resistance placed in series with the relay).

A track relay.

The arrows show the direction of current flow. Starting from positive post of the battery, the current flows through the limiting resistance, the one rail the relay windings, the relay series resistance, and the other rail, then back to the negative post of the battery. With the relay energized, it closes a contact to light the lamps (or to control mechanism).

The wheels and the axles of the train are conductive. This means that when the wheels of the train come in contact with the track section, the circuit shorts out. As the wheels and axles of a train move onto the track circuit, they provide a path from rail to rail through which the battery current flows, thus robbing the relay of its current and causing it to open the contact.

In other words, when no train is present, the relay is energized by the current flowing from the power source through the rails. When a train is present, its axles shorten (shunt) the rails together, the current to the track relay coil drops, and the relay is de-energized. Therefore circuits through the relay contacts report whether or not the track is occupied.

A track has the ability to carry current. A track section is a piece of a track that is isolated, so that the current does not spread from one track section to another. This means that track sections can carry current independently of each other. Each track section is connected to a relay. The only external influences on the track section that will affect the state of the relay is a train or other conductive components.

2.1.2 Signal Relay

Signal relay is a general term for all kinds of relays in railway signal. Relays are widely used in railway signal technology, and relays are indispensable components of various signal control systems.

A relay is an electrical excitation switch, which is an electromagnet with contacts. The relay consists of two main parts: electromagnetic system and contact system. The electromagnetic system consists of coils, fixed iron cores, a yoke iron and a movable magnet armature. The contact system includes movable contacts and static contacts. When a certain value of current passed coils, an electromagnetic attraction produced by electromagnetic interaction or induction method attracts the magnet armature. The magnet armature drives the contact system and changes its state to reflect the status of the input current.

The electromagnetic relay is shown in figure 2.2. When a certain value of current passed coils, a certain amount of flux produced between the magnet armature and iron-core goes through the iron core, magnet armature, yoke iron and air gap to form a closed magnetic circuit. And then the iron core produces an attraction for magnet armature. The size of the attraction depends on the value of the current. When the current increases to a certain value, the increasing attraction can be able to overcome the resistance of

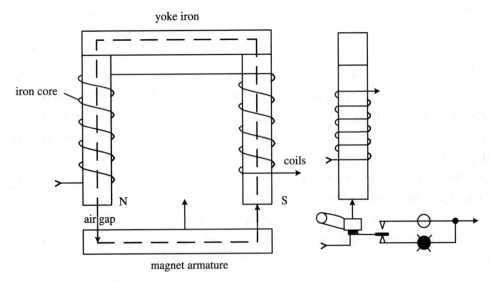

Figure 2.2 The basic principle of the electromagnetic relay

the magnet armature moving to the iron core (mainly the magnet armature's own gravity), and the magnet armature is attracted to the iron core. The movable contacts which are driven by the magnet armature (contacts along with the moving magnet armature) also move, and connect with the movable close contacts (front contacts). This state is called relay excitation.

The attraction decreases with the decrease of the current. When the decreasing attraction is not enough to overcome the magnet armature's own gravity, the magnet armature by reason of its gravity drop down (called release). The magnet armature drives the movable contacts to disconnect with front contacts, and then connects with movable break contacts (back contacts). This state is called relay excitation-loss.

It can be seen that the relay has the switching characteristics, which can be used to connect and break the circuit to form various control and indication circuits.

2.1.3 Signal

In order to indicate the commands of train running and shunting operation, it is necessary to set up all kinds of signals and signal indicators as required in the railway. They are the indispensable components invarious signal systems, which are used to form signal displays for operating conditions. The color light signal is signaled by the color, number, and state of the lighting. This article only introduces LED signal.

The LED signal display system has been successfully used as new type of light source, which has the characteristics of energy saving and maintenance-free.

The display distance of the LED signal is more than 1.5 km and it is clear and reliable. The monitoring control system can monitor the working state of the signal, and the warning abnormity can help to accurately determine the fault point and facilitate timely processing. The LED signal can be greatly reduced in weight, which is easy to install. It has a good sealing condition and long service life, which can reach 10^5 h, using the LED to replace the traditional double filament signal light bulb and the lens group can eliminate the filament burnout, which is the multiple signal failure. It has high reliability, stable focus, good luminosity, no impact current and no maintenance. It ends the maintenance workload and saves maintenance cost.

The LED railway signal is composed of the signal mechanism of aluminum alloy, luminous panel and its special lighting device. The signal mechanism of aluminum alloy is divided into high post and dwarf mechanism.

The luminous panel is a new light source, which use slight emitting diodes. The luminous panel is divided into high post, dwarf and indicator luminous panel. The luminous panel is a circular disk with many light emitting diodes. The special lighting device of luminous panel is signal lighting device for the development of luminous panel. The device is not only stable and reliable, but also can be used for large range of voltage fluctuation.

2.1.4 Axle Counter

An axle counter is a system consisting of counting points at both ends of a section and a counter connected to the counting points (figure 2.3).

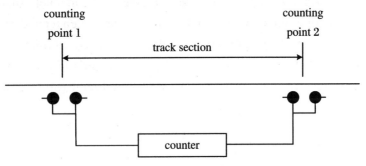

Figure 2.3 Axle counter

A counting head (or detection point) is installed at each end of the section, and as each axle passes the head at the start of the section, a counter increments. A detection point comprises two independent sensors, therefore the device can detect the direction of a train by the order in which the sensors are passed. As the train passes a similar counting head at the end of the section, the counter decrements.

The occupancy of a section is detected by comparing the number of axles which enter the section with the number of axle which leave the section. To give a clear indication, the parity of number is necessary. Counting points are usually made up of double contacts to detect the direction of movement. This is necessary to avoid counting too many axles in case of an axle swinging over a counting point while the train is not in motion.

2.1.5 Switch Machine

The switch is the key equipment which directly relates to the train operation safety. It is easy to centralize control and realize automation to convert and lock by various switch machines. The switch machine is an important signal basic equipment, which plays a very important role in ensuring the train operation safety, increasing the transportation efficiency and relieving the labor intensity of the train staff. The following is a brief introduction to several commonly used switching machines.

ZD6-A type electric switch machine mainly consists of the motor, retarder, friction coupling, main axle, throw rod, indication rod, switch circuit controller, shifting contactor, body case and so on. The motor provides power for the electric switch machine, which use DC series motor.

The S700K type electric switch machine is due to the need of speed up, through introduction, absorption and improvement of the foreign switch machine. This type switch machine structure is advanced with sophisticated technology, which not only solved the inertia failures of the motor wire broken, fault current changed, bad contact, shifting contactor jumped up, dissectible pin broken and so on, but also can do it "less maintenance, no maintenance". The S700K type electric switch machine is mainly composed of the shell, power driving mechanism, detection and locking mechanism, safety device and wiring interface. The three-phase AC motor provides power for the switch machine.

The ZD (J) 9 series electric switch machine is developed for the acceleration of Chinese railway. A series of products are developed according to the different switching stroke and force of the switch and the AC and DC power supply modes. It has the characteristics of big switching force and high efficiency. It can be used for the conversion of external locking switches with multi-point traction, and it can also be used for the conversion of inside locking switches with switch tongue linkage.

The ZD (J) 9 series electric switch machine adopts the ball screw to slow down, which is more efficient. The AC series adopts the three-phase 380 V AC motor, which has the characteristics of less faults and long control distance of signal core cable. A DC series switch can be configured as required.

2.2 Block System

2.2.1 Manual Block System

In a manual block system the clearance of block sections has to be checked by local operators by watching the rear end train markers. The block signals are operated manually, the block information is transmitted by means of telecommunications, in its most simple form by telephone (telephone block).

On single track lines, a train which is going to leave a station has to be offered to the next station where the train sequence may be changed. This receiving station can be a junction or a station with passing tracks. After this receiving station has accepted the train. All intermediate block sections will be reserved for this train. When the train has departed, the time of departure is transmitted to the receiving station and also to all intermediate block stations. After the train has cleared a block section and is protected by a stop signal, a clearance messages is being sent to the block section in rear. On double track lines where a current of traffic is in effect, offering and accepting of trains is only required for movements against the current of traffic. All train movements and train messages are recorded by the station operators in a hand written train record.

2.2.2 Semi-automatic Block System

In semi-automatic block system the signals are still operated manually but are controlled by continuous track circuits, requiring cooperation between the operators of adjacent block stations. A signal cannot be cleared when the block section is occupied by a train or when the operator at the adjacent block section has cleared a signal for an opposing movement. Checking the train integrity by watching the rear end train markers is not necessary.

The block instruments are interlocked with the signals in a block apparatus. After a train has entered the block section, the signal is locked by a block instrument in stop position, thus preventing the operator from clearing the signal again until he has received tile clearance information from the operator of the next signal.

2.2.3 Automatic Block System

In an automatic block territory the occupation and clearance of block sections and overlaps is detected by a track clear detection device to enable the signaling system to work automatically. Therefore, there is no need to have local operators to check the train integrity by watching the rear end markers. On single track lines and on double track lines with two ways working the automatic block system also provides protection against opposing movements.

Compared with the semi-automatic block system, ABS has many advantages:

① Because the section between the two stations allows the continuation of train tracking operation, it greatly improves the driving density and significantly improves the carrying capacity of the section.

② Because there is no need for blocking procedures, it simplifies the procedure for departure and receiving trains, thus improving the carrying capacity, and greatly reducing the labor intensity of the station attendants.

③ Because the display of the block signal can directly reflect the location of the train and the state of the line, it ensures the safety of the train operation in the section.

2.2.4 Fixed Block

Today, signal operations with a fixed block system is common form of operation.

Signaling with line side signals is still typical. But there is also an increasing use of cab signal system, especially on high speed lines where lineside signals cannot be watched safely. The fixed block system only allows the following train to move up to the last unoccupied block's border. A fixed block system is a block system using fixed block sections which are protected by signals (lineside or cab signals). To clear a signal for a train that is to enter a block section, the following conditions must have been fulfilled:

① The train ahead must have cleared the block section.

② The train ahead must have cleared the overlap behind the next signal (only on lines where block overlaps are used).

③ The train ahead must be protected from following train movements by a stop signal.

④ The train is protected against opposing movements.

On railways where block overlaps are not required, the control length of a signal equals the block section. Examples are mainline railway in North America and in Russia. Other railways require a control length of a signal that is longer than the block section (figure 2.4). The difference is called "overlap" because in that area the control length of a signal overlaps with the control length of the next signal. The main purpose of the overlap is to provide additional safety in case the driver fails to brake before a stop signal. A signal may not be cleared until the full control length is clear. Thus, the clearing point

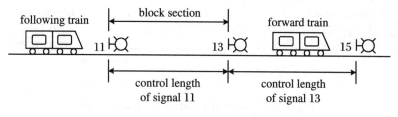

(a) Line without block overlaps

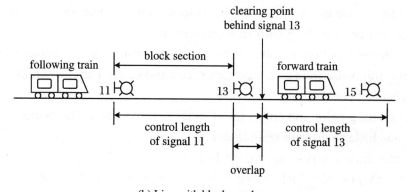

(b) Line with block overlaps

Figure 2.4　Control length of signals in a fixed block territory behind a signal equals the end of the control length of the signal in rear. Block overlaps are used on all European railways, many railways outside of Europe and also on almost all subways and subway-like electric city railways worldwide.

2.2.5 Moving Block

The moving block is a signaling system where the safe tracking intervals are defined in real time as the train movement instead of being defined in advance, is a new type blocking system. which overcomes the weaknesses of fixed block. The Communication Based Train Control (CBTC) is one of the main technical means.

Moving block can be implemented by track-mounted induction loops or wireless communication. Early moving block systems are mostly based on track-mounted induction loops, namely train positioning and the continuous communication between VOBC and VCC. But now, the communications between sub-systems are implemented by wireless communication in most advanced moving block systems.

In a moving block system as shown in the figure 2.5, the train position and its braking curve is continuously calculated by the trains, and then communicated via radio to the wayside equipment. Thus, the wayside equipment is able to establish protected areas, each one called Limit of Movement Authority (LMA), up to the nearest obstacle.

Figure 2.5 Schematic diagram of moving block

The features of moving block are as follows:

① The tracks are not divided into fixed block sections. The intervals between trains are dynamic and change along with train movement.

② The interval between trains is calculated according to the braking distance required by the following train at the current speed and safety margin. Train intervals ensure that trains do not rear-end.

③ The starting point and end point of braking is dynamic. The number of trackside equipment has little to do with train intervals.

④ Smaller train intervals can be smaller.

⑤ Two-way ground-vehicle transmission is adopted. Large amount of information can be transmitted, and unmanned driving can be achieved more easily.

The moving block system measures distance of the train and forward train continuously, provides the information of train position, speed and acceleration and controls train running speed dynamically. The max braking target can be closer to the forward train in moving block system, which means the train intervals can be reduced. Therefore, it is easy to achieve small group and high density, and reduce passenger waiting time, platform width and space and infrastructure investment. The number of hardware is greatly reduced due to the system is modular designed and the core part is implemented by software. Therefore, it can save maintenance costs. The fundamental difference between moving block and fixed block is the way to forming block sections.

Moving block goes a further step in controlling safe interval between trains. The control center can calculate max train braking distance according real time speed and position through the two-way communication between onboard equipment and trackside equipment. A virtual section equaling to the sum of train length, max braking distance and a safe distance is formed, which moves synchronously with the train. Two adjacent moving block section can move forward synchronously at small intervals, which makes trains can run at high speed and small intervals and improves operation efficiency.

2.2.6 Three-aspect and Four-aspect Automatic Block System

As shown in figure 2.6, an automatic block section is usually divided into a number of small sections between stations, which is called block section. A block signal is installed at the entrance (starting end) of each block section.

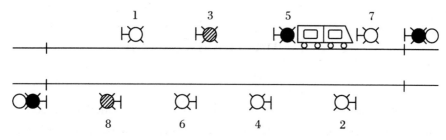

Figure 2.6 The schematic of the automatic block system

The block signals of three-aspect automatic block section use the three-aspect mechanism, and the top down is yellow, green and red light. It can predict the state of two block sections ahead of the train. When the green light is on, the train is allowed to run at the given speed, indicating that at least two block sections are free in the front. When the yellow light is on, the train is required to pay attention to the operation, indicating that there is only one block section is free. When the red light is on, the train must stop at the signal (figure 2.7).

Four-aspect automatic block is the addition of green and yellow light on the basis of three-aspect automatic block, which can predict the state of three block sections ahead. The signal mechanism still adopts three-aspect, and the top down is green, red and yellow lights. The green and yellow light indicates that two block sections ahead of the train are free. When the green light is on, it indicates that there are three or more block section are free. The yellow light and the red light show the same meaning as the three-aspect system (figure 2.8).

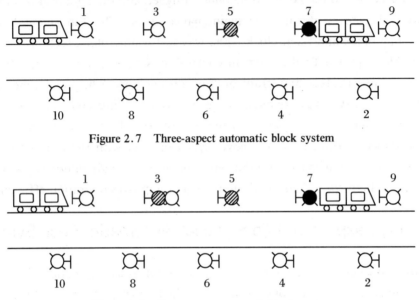

Figure 2.7　Three-aspect automatic block system

Figure 2.8　Four-aspect automatic block system

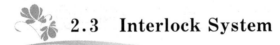 2.3　Interlock System

Interlocking is the mutual restrictive relationship established by technical means among signals, switches and routes. The fundamental contents of urban rail transit interlocking contain: prevent the set of the route that would cause the rolling stockto collide; all the switched that one train goes through are locked at the positions corresponding to the route open direction; the display of the signal must match the established route.

Interlocking is an important technical measure to ensure the safety of driving. It refers to the restrictive relationship between signal equipment and related factors. The generalized interlocking refers to the mutual constraint relationship of various signal devices. The narrowly defined interlocking refers to the restrictive relationship between routes, signals, and switches within the station.

For urban rail transit, the "station" includes the mainline station and the depot/parking. To ensure safe operation, the interlocking relationship must be very strict. An arrangement of signals and appliances is interconnected so that their movements must succeed each other in proper sequence and for which interlocking rules are in effect. It may be operated manually or automatically.

Interlocking can be categorized as all-mechanical, electrical (relay-based), and electronic/computer-based.

2.3.1 Interlocking Principles

Firstly, "an interlocking" is the interlocking plant where points and signals are interconnected in a way that each movement follow the other in a proper and safe sequence. Secondly, the principles to achieve a safe interconnection between points and signals are also generally called "interlocking".

The route a train could use through an interlocking must meet the following conditions:

① All points must be set properly and locked.
② Conflicting routes must be locked.
③ The track must be clear.

This is provided by the following functions:

① Interlocking between points and signals.
② Route locking.
③ Locking conflicting routes.
④ Flank protection.
⑤ Track clear detection.

2.3.2 Relay Interlocking

In relay interlocking the full function is realized by relay circuitry without any mechanical elements. The development of all relay interlocking started in the 1920s.

In past systems, relay circuits provide the interlocking. When the operator of the interlocking is located within the locality of the interlocked switches and signals, controls are directed by wire, and central energy sources are provided to operate the relays, signals and electric switch machines. Energy sources are common batteries of storage cells, with provision for charging from commercial power which is available. Sometimes standby power sources, such as motor generator sets, are also provided. When one — or sometimes several — locations are distant from the control center, remote control and indication systems are used. There are many types of remote control systems, some use physical line circuits, some carrier, some microwave, etc.

Relay interlocking is also controlled via keyboards and video monitors, but the basic relay interlocking circuits remain the same. The track diagram in the upper portion of the panel represents the track layout.

2.3.3 Computer Based Interlocking

Relay interlocking was widely used due to its steady property. While, its logic circuits are composed by relays, which is difficult to express and implement complex logic relations. Therefore, the functions of relay interlocking are not perfect, and it is a lack of security. It also lacks flexibility of communications with modern information system. It will be replaced by higher level interlocking system — Computer Based Interlocking (CBI). England from 1984 started to develop computer-based interlocking system, at present, as the core railway transportation safety control system, replacing the original 6502 Electric.

CBI (also called CI) is a real-time control system which is composed by microcomputers, some other electronic devices and relays. It has technical and economic advantages when compared with relay interlocking. And its design, construction, maintenance and utilization are more convenient than relay interlocking.

The main differences between CBI and relay interlocking are as follow:

① CBI performs logic calculations of station attendant's commands and the indication information of field supervision devices by microcomputers to accomplish the interlocks between signals, switches and routes. All interlocking relations are realized by microcomputer and its programs.

② Control commands from microcomputers and indication information from field devices are all transmitted serially by transmission channel. This saves a lot of trunk cable, and makes the use of fiber optic cable transmission possible.

③ Computer-based interlocking uses screen instead of control panel, which shrinks the system volume, riches display information, simplifies the structure and improves usability. Display and operation are divided in CBI, and variable operations are used together to avoid system paralysis caused by equipment failure.

④ Modular building design of hardware and software makes it easy to change station and realize the function of fault detection analysis.

CBI systems can be divided into human-machine level, interlocking level and supervision level. And the functions of these levels can be realized by HMI (Human-Machine Interface), interlocking computer and controllers (they also can be called concentrator) respectively. Therefore, the whole system can be divided into two levels, namely human-machine level and interlocking level. The structure is depicted by figure 2.9.

(1) Human-machine Computer

Human-machine computer (HM computer) receives the operation input from, control panel and judges whether the input is valid or not. If valid, HM computer converts the input into predetermined format, and transmits it to interlocking computer. In addition, HM computer receives indication information from interlocking computer and converts it into the style that can be accepted by indicator or control panel.

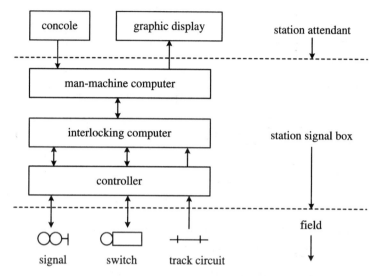

Figure 2.9 Structure diagram of CBI system

(2) **Interlocking Computer**

Interlocking computer receives operation orders and status information of field devices from human-machine computer, and sends the control orders of converting switches and clearing signals after interlocking logic calculations.

(3) **Controllers**

The connections between field object group and indoor interlocking computer are realized by controller. It receives control codes and forms control orders to drive control circuits. It also receives status information about supervised objects and transmits to the interlocking computer after coding. It reserves the field devices adopted electrical centralization.

The software of CBI is composed by three function packages, namely human-machine dialogue processing, interlocking logic and execution and indication. And software packages are communicated by professional system management software.

Mostly, CBI employs redundant structures to improve reliability and safety. Redundant structures of CBI systems can be divided into two hot standby, 3-to-2 and 2×2-2 according the redundancy of interlocking system.

In 3-to-2 systems, the results of 3 CPUs are compared respectively, and when two of them are the same (including the situation that the three results are the same), the system can work normally, The structure of 3-to-2 system is depicted in figure 2.10. The 3-to-2 system cannot satisfy the maintenance requirement of CBI system. So, the 3-to-2

CBI systems are not developed any longer.

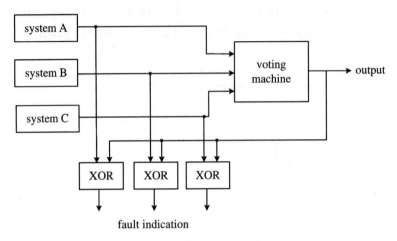

Figure 2.10　Diagram of 3-to-2 system

In 2×2 to 2 system, 2 CPUs constitute a sub-system (host machine) to execute interlock tasks, another 2 CPUs operate in hot standby state, In 2×2 to 2 system, host machine uses 2 CPUs that execute interlocking programs coding differently, and operations of 2 CPUs are compared to detect faults. Figure 2.11 shows the structure of 2×2-to-2. So far, the 2×2-to-2 CBI is widely used.

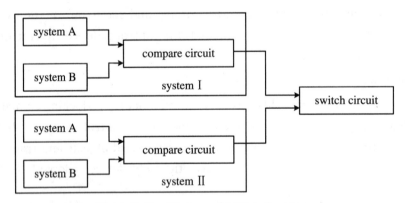

Figure 2.11　Diagram of 2 × 2-to-2 systems

2.3.4　The Fundamental Contents of Interlocking

The fundamental contents of interlocking contain: prevent the set of the route that would cause the rolling stock to collide; all the switched that one train goes through are locked at the positions corresponding to the route open direction; the display of the signal must match the established route.

① The signal can only be opened when the route is vacant.

One of the most basic interlocking conditions is the signal can only be opened when the route is vacant. If the sections (the mainline is the interlock monitoring section) occupied by one train is arranged to one route, the relevant train signal cannot be opened. If the sections are occupied and the signal is opened, it will cause the train or the shunting train to collide with the original train.

As shown in figure 2.12, 2DG, 4-6DG and 4 G must be vacant if route SC to Z_4 is to be set up.

② The signal can be opened only when the switches related to the route are locked in the correct position.

The signal can be opened only when the switches related to the route are locked in the correct position. This is one of the most basic interlocking conditions. The signal protecting one route cannot be opened if the position of any switch is not correct or the point of any switch is not closely attached to its basic track. If the position of any switch is not correct, it will cause the train enters to the wrong track or damages the switch. The switches related to the route are locked in the specified positions after the signal is opened and cannot be converted.

As shown in figure 2.12, the switch 2 must be at reverse, the switch 4 and 6 must be at normal if a route SC to Z_4 is to set.

③ The signal can be opened when its hostile signals are not open and are locked in the off state.

The signal cannot be opened when its hostile signals are open. This is one of the most basic interlocking conditions. When the hostile route is not unlocked or the inspection conditions are not matched, the signal that protects the route cannot be opened. Otherwise, head-on collisions may happen between trains. The hostile signals are locked in the off state and cannot be opened after the signal is opened.

As shown in figure 2.12, the signal F_5 must be in off state if a route SC to Z_1 is to set.

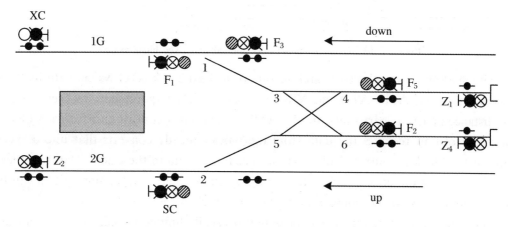

Figure 2.12 Centralized station in mainline

2.4 Automatic Train Control System

2.4.1 ATC

The letters ATC refer to "Automatic Train Control", where the system includes ATP (Automatic Train Protection), ATO (Automatic Train Operation) and ATS (Automatic Train Supervision). It has been adopted around the world to describe the architecture of the automatically operated railway. Of course, it is usually applied only to metros.

There are a number of ways to assemble the parts of an ATC package, but a common format used by many systems looks like figure 2.13.

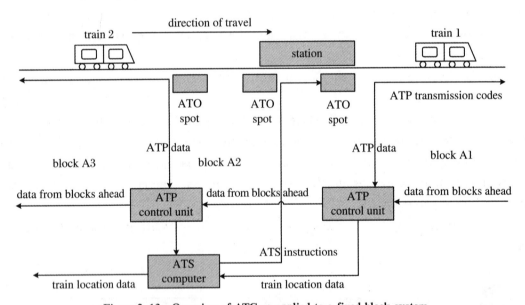

Figure 2.13 Overview of ATC as applied to a fixed block system

The diagram shows the basic architecture of a fixed block ATC system with its three main components: ATP, ATO and ATS. The basic safely requirement, to keep trains a safe distance apart, is performed by the ATP, which has a control unit for each block. Train control unit receives the data from the blocks ahead, converts that into a speed limit for the block it controls and sends the speed limit data to the track. The train picks up the data using the codes transmitted along the track. The transmission system can be track circuits, loops or beacons located along the track.

The data received by the ATP control unit is usually limited to indicating that a train is in the block or the speed limit currently imposed in the block. This data is sent to the

ATS computer where it is compared with the timetable to determine if the train is running according to schedule or is late or early. To adjust the train's timing, the ATS can send commands to the ATO spots located along the track.

The ATO spots, which can be short transmission loops or small boxes called beacons, give the train its station stop commands. The spots usually contain fixed data but some, usually the last one in a station stop sequence, transmit data about the time the train should stop (the dwell time) at the station and may tell it how fast to go to the next station (ATP permitting).

Some systems leave the ATO spots alone, they use the ATP system to prevent the train from starting or restrict its speed because their data is always fixed. The ATS computer tells the ATP control unit to transmit a restricted speed or zero speed to the track.

Both ATP and ATO commands are picked up by aerials on the train and translated into motoring, braking or coasting commands. Where a train can be manually driven, the ATP will still ensure the safety requirement but the ATO is overridden, the driver stopping the train in the stations by use of the cab controls.

There are lots of variations of ATC around the world, but all contain the basic principle that ATP provides safety and is the basis upon which the train is allowed to run. ATO provides controls to replace the driver, while ATS checks the running times and adjusts train running accordingly.

There is little difference between fixed block and moving block as far as ATC is concerned, but the architecture will look something like figure 2.14.

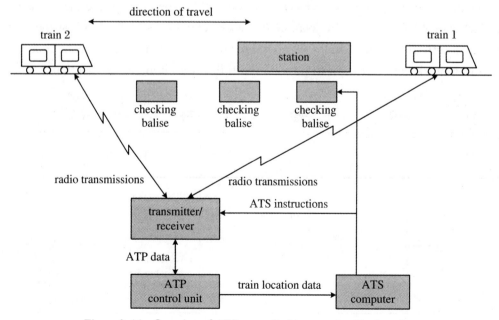

Figure 2.14 Overview of ATS as applied to a moving block system

The transmission of data to the rails is gone and is replaced by radio transmission. Also, there are no blocks. The train's location is determined by the on-board route map, which is reset when the train starts its trip and is verified by "checking balise" spaced along the route. The balise can be used to send ATS instructions to the train, but like the ATO spots used in fixed block systems, they contain static data about location and route profile.

In a moving block system, the ATP control unit differs from that used in a fixed block system. It now covers a larger area and it gets its data from the radio transmissions. It sends data by radio as well. If the radio transmission fails to reach a train, this train assumes that the train in front has stopped at its last known position and will stop a safe distance behind it.

ATS covers the same functions as for fixed block systems. Train location data is received and train running adjusted as necessary. In all ATS systems nowadays, there is lots of data logging to provide management information and statistics and some ATS systems allow replays of sections of the day's train movements to assist in formulating future management strategies.

2.4.2 ATP

This section introduced two kinds of ATP, one is ATP based on fixed block, and another is ATP based on distance-to-go.

To adapt metro signaling to modem, electronic ATP, the overlaps are incorporated into the block system. This is done by counting the block behind an occupied block as the overlap. Thus, in a full, fixed block ATP system, there will be two red signals and an unoccupied, or overlap block between train to provide the full safe braking distance (figure 2.15).

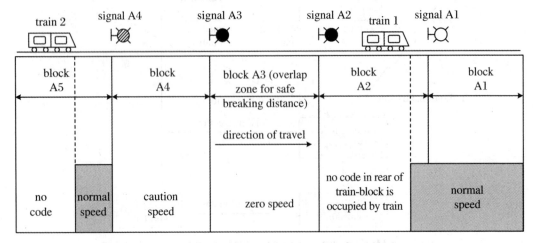

Figure 2.15　Diagram of ATP based on fixed block

On a line equipped with ATP as shown above, each block carries an electronic speed code on top of its track circuit. If the train tries to enter a zero speed block or an occupied block, or if it enters a section at a speed higher than that authorized by the code, the on-board electronics will cause an emergency brake application.

A train on a line with a modem version of ATP needs two pieces of information about the state of the line ahead what speed can it do in this block and what speed must it be doing by the time it enter the next block. This speed data is picked up by antennae on the train. The data is coded by the electronic equipment controlling the track circuit and transmitted from the rails. The code data consists of two parts, the authorized speed code for this block and the target speed code for the next block. Figure 2.16 shows how it works.

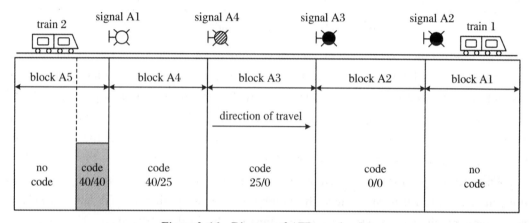

Figure 2.16 Diagram of ATP speed codes

In this example, a train in block A5 approaching signal A4 will receive 40 over code (40/40) to indicate a permitted speed of 40 km/h in this block and a target speed of 40 km/h for the next. This is the normal speed data. However, when it enter block A4, the code will change to 40/25 because the target speed must be 25 km/h when the train enters the next block A3. When the train enters block A3, the code change again to 25/0 because the next block A2 is the overlap block and is forbidden territory, so the speed must be zero by the time train reaches the end of block A3. If the train attempts to enter block A2, the on-board equipment will be detect the zero speed code (0/0) and will cause an emergency brake application. As mentioned above, block A2 is acting as the overlap or safe braking distance behind the train occupying block Al.

Train operating over a line equipment with ATP can be manually or automatically driven. To allow manual driving, the ATP codes are displayed to the driver on a panel in his cab. In our example below (figure 2.17), the driver would begin braking somewhere around the brake initiation point because he would see the 40/25 code on his display and would know, from his knowledge of the line, where he will have to stop. If signals are not provided, the signal positions will normally be indicated by trackside block marker boards to show drivers the entrances to blocks.

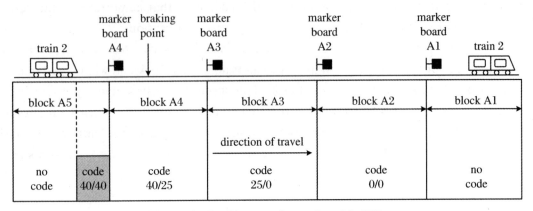

Figure 2.17　Diagram of operation with ATP

For the distance-to-go system, the development of modem electronics has allowed the brake curve to be monitored continuously. When it enters the first block with a speed restriction in the code, the train is also told how far ahead the stopping point is. The on-board computer knows where the train is now, using the line "map" embedded in its memory, and it calculates the required braking curve accordingly. As the train brakes, the computer checks the progress down the curve to check the train never goes outside it.

Distance-to-go ATP has a number of advantages. As we have seen, it can increase line capacity but also it can reduce the number of track circuit required, since you don't need frequent changes of steps to keep adjusting the braking distance. The blocks are now just the spaces to be occupied by train and are not used overlaps as well. Distance-to-go can be used for manual driving or automatic operation.

System varies but often, usually there are some necessary curves which are provided for the train braking profile. This example shows three: one is normal curve within which the train should brake, the second is a warning curve, which provides a warning to the driver (an audio-visual alarm or a service brake application depending on the system) and the third is the emergency curve which will force an emergency brake if the driver does not reduce speed to within the emergency braking curve (figure 2.18).

2.4.3　ATO

The basic requirement of ATO is to tell the train approaching a station where to stop so that the complete train is in the platform. This is assuming that the ATP has confirmed that the line is clear. The sequence operates as show figure 2.19.

The train approaches the station under clear signals so it can do a normal run in. When it reaches the first beacon — originally a looped cable, now usually a fixed transponder — a station brake command is received by the train. The on board computer calculates the braking curve to enable it to stop at the correct point and, as the train runs in towards the platform, the curve is updated a number of times (it varies from system to system) to ensure accuracy.

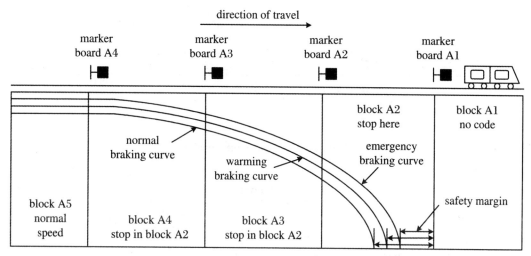

Figure 2.18   Diagram of operation with distance-to-go

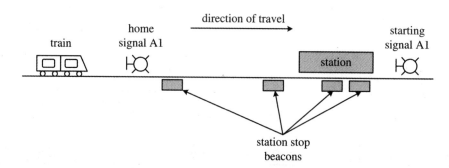

Figure 2.19   The train approaching a station

To provide a frequent train service on a metro, dwell times at stations must be kept to a minimum. In spite of the best endeavors of staff, trains sometimes overstay their time at stations, so signaling was been developed to reduce the impact on following trains. To see how this works, we begin with an example (figure 2.20) of a conventionally signaled station with a starting signal A1 (green) and a home signal A2 (red) protecting a train (train 1) standing in the station. We can assume mechanical ATP (train stops) is provided so the overlap of signal A2 is a full speed braking distance in advance of the platform.

As train 2 approaches, it slows when the driver sees the home signal A2 at danger. Even if train 1 then starts and begins to leave the station, signal A2 will remain at danger until train 1 has cleared the overlap of signal A1. Train 2 will have to stop at A2 but will then restart almost immediately when signal A2 clears. This causes a delay to train 2 and it requires more energy to restart the train. A way was found to allow the second train to keep moving, it is called multi-home signaling (figure 2.21).

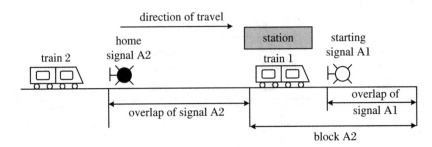

Figure 2.20　Single-home signaling

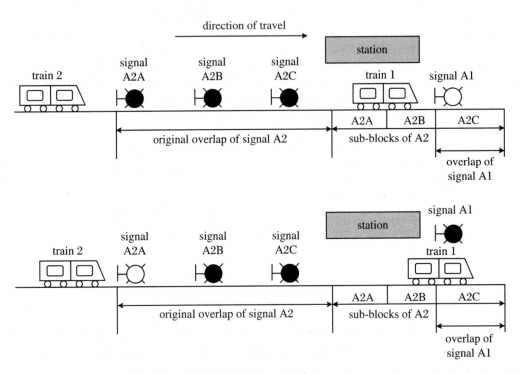

Figure 2.21　Multi-home signaling system

Where multi-home signaling is installed at a station, it involves the provision of more but shorter blocks, each with its own signal. The original home signal in our example has become signal A2A and, while train 1 is in the platform, it will remain at danger. However, block A2 is broken up into three smaller sub-blocks, A2A, A2B, and A2C, each with its own signal. They will also be at danger while train 1 is in the platform. Train 2 is approaching and beginning to brake so as to stop at signal A2A. When train 1 begins to leave the station, it will clear sub-block A2A first and signal A2A will then show green. Train 2 will have reduced speed somewhat but can now begin its run in towards the platform.

At this next stage in the sequence, we can see (figure 2.22) that train 1 has now cleared two sub-blocks, A2A and A2B, so two of the multi-home signals are now clear. Note that the starting signal is now red as the train has entered the next block A1. Train 2 is running towards the station at a reduced speed but it has not had to stop. When train 1 clears the overlap of signal A1, the whole of block A2 is clear and signal A2C clears to allow train 2 an unobstructed run into the platform.

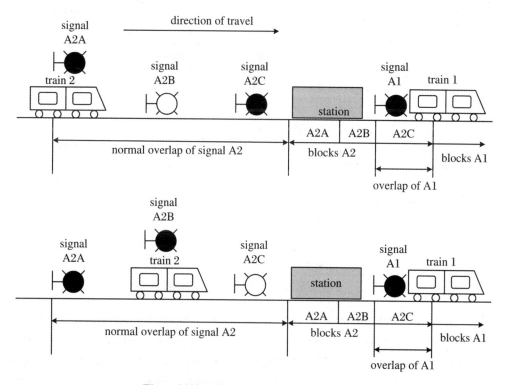

Figure 2.22 Multi-home signaling — run in

Fixed block metro systems use multi-home signaling with ATO and ATP (figure 2.23). A series of sub-blocks are provided in the platform area. These impose reduced speed braking curves on the incoming train and allow it to run towards the platform as the preceding train departs, whilst keeping a safe braking distance between them. Each curve represents a sub-block. Enforcement is carried out by the ATP system monitoring the train speed. The station stop beacons still give the train the data for the braking curve for the station stop, but the train will recalculate the curve to compensate for the lower speed imposed by the ATP system.

ATO systems take door operation away from the operator and give it to the ATO system, so equipment is provided as shown in figure 2.24.

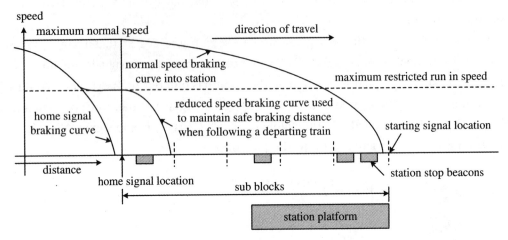

Figure 2.23 ATO/ATP multi home signaling

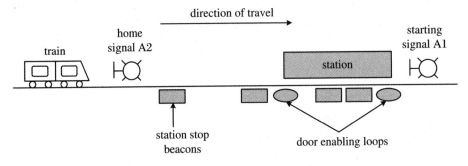

Figure 2.24 Docking and starting

When the train has stopped, it verifies that its brakes are applied and checks that it has stopped within the door enabling loops. These loops verify the position of the train relative to the platform and which side the doors should open. Once all this is complete, the ATO will open the doors. After a set time, predetermined or varied by the control center as required, the ATO will close the doors and automatically restart the train if the door closed proving circuit is complete. Platform screen doors and door achieve interconnected open and close.

2.4.4 ATS

ATS system is commonly integrated within most of the CBTC solutions. Its main task is to act as the interface between the operator and the system, mana-ging the traffic according to the specific regulation criteria.

General, a CBTC may interface to, or be integrated with, an ATS system. Under such circumstances, CBTC-related ATS functions shall be implemented in order to benefit from the characteristics of a CBTC system namely:

① Availability of train location information to a high precision, indepen-dent of track circuits.

② Availability of continuous wayside-to-train and train-to-wayside data communications link.

③ Availability of train borne and wayside data processing capabilities.

Each ATS user interface shall display all information and implement all control actions as defined, within acceptable latencies. The ATS user shall be able to override any automated CBTC related ATS functions.

Each CBTC-equipped train operating within CBTC territory shall be assigned a train identification. This train identification shall indicate the type of train and other pertinent information about the train. The following mainly introduces its functions.

① An ATS system shall have the capability to automatically track, maintain records of, and display on the ATS user interface the locations, identities, train schedule, and other pertinent data for all CBTC-equipped trains operating in the CBTC territory. The front and rear position of trains shall be tracked based on CBTC train location reports, and displayed on the ATS user interface. Variations in train length may be displayed either proportionally or as a standard length icon supplemented by textural train length data.

② An ATS system shall have the capability to permit CBTC-equipped trains operating in CBTC territory to be manually and automatically routed based on CBTC train location reports and in accordance with the train service data, predefined routing rules, and any ATS user directed service strategy. Automatic routing shall facilitate the proper merging and diverging of trains at junctions, turnback of trains, the put-in and lay-up of trains from/to storage areas and, where applicable, the rerouting of trains in response to service disruptions and/or planned outages. Train routes shall be indicated on the ATS user interface.

③ An ATS system shall also include a means to control and limit movement authorities of CBTC-equipped trains operating in CBTC territory. CBTC movement authority limits shall be capable of being displayed on the ATS user interface, and any uncommanded reductions of authority limits shall be alarmed.

④ An ATS system shall have the capability to automatically monitor and regulate the performance of CBTC equipped trains operating in CBTC territory, in relation to schedule and/or headway adherence.

⑤ An ATS system shall include an automatic dispatching function (based on train identities, CBTC train location reports, scheduled and actual headways between trains, and service strategies implemented by authorized ATS users). Schedule and headway regulation for CBTC-equipped trains shall be by means of dwell time variance (including train holds), and control of run-times between stations. When operating in ATO mode, shall be implemented automatically by a CBTC system using the automatic speed regulation function. An ATS system may provide the capability to adjust the train service braking profiles for CBTC-equipped trains. A CBTC system shall coordinate implementation of requested changes in service braking profiles to avoid conditions that would result in an emergency brake application.

⑥ An ATS system may have the capability to implement energy optimization algorithms for CBTC equipped trains through the real-time control and coordination of train acceleration, train coasting, and train braking.

⑦ An ATS system may include the means to direct a single CBTC-equipped train or a group of CBTC-equipped trains to stop at the next station, even if the train is scheduled to by passing that station. A CBTC system shall indicate the ATS train stop information to the train operator and conductor on their displays. In ATO mode, a CBTC-equipped train shall automatically stop at the next station.

⑧ An ATS system may include facilities to hold (and subsequently release) a CBTC-equipped train at a station, and to inhibit automatic train door opening. A CBTC system shall indicate the train hold information to the train operator and conductor on their displays, and shall prevent a CBTC-equipped train from departing the station in ATO mode.

⑨ An ATS system may include facilities to direct a CBTC-equipped train or group of CBTC-equipped trains to pass through a station or group of stations without stopping. A CBTC system shall indicate the skip station information to the train operator and conductor on their displays. In ATO mode, the train shall automatically skip the designated stations.

2.5 Communication Based Train Control System

CBTC is a railway signaling system that makes use of the telecommunications between the train and track equipment for the traffic management and infrastructure control. CBTC adopts induction communication or wireless communication technology to realize the two-way and large capacity train-trackside information transmission. It is a new type of train control system, which is the best technical means to realize moving block system, achieves the purpose of continuous communication and closed-up control of train running.

CBTC comprehensively uses 3C technology (computer technology, communication technology and control technology) to replace the track circuit, and realizes the closed-loop control of the train operation in the real sense. Using induction communication or wireless communication can achieve the purpose of continuous communication, which can provide continuous train safety interval guarantee and over-speed protection. It has better accuracy and greater flexibility in the train control, and can detect fault points faster. Moreover, moving block can adjust the length of the block section according to the actual and relative speed of the train, minimize the operation interval of the train as much as possible, and improve the train density. In addition, compared with the traditional system, this system will greatly reduce equipment along the line, easy installation and maintenance, and help to reduce operating costs.

The basic feature of CBTC is that there are various types of wireless two-way communication between the train and the trackside.

CBTC is a moving block type train control system with advanced communication and computer technology, continuous control and monitoring of train operation, and based on "communication", which represents the development trend of train control system in the world. It breaks away from the limitation of fixed (or quasi-moving) block section by using track circuit to distinguish whether the section is occupied or not. Compared with the previous system, it has greater advantages, which are embodied as follows:

① It realizes the real-time two-way and large capacity communication between the train and the trackside equipment.

② It can reduce the trackside equipment and facilitate the installation and maintenance, which is conducive to the use of the line as evacuation channels in emergency situations, and help to reduce the operating cost of the system within the life cycle.

③ It is convenient to shorten the train marshalling and high-density operation, shorten the length of platform and end rail, improve the service quality and reduce the investment of civil engineering. The realization of double direction operation of the train without increasing the trackside equipment, is conducive to the reverse operation control when the track failure happened or for some special needs.

④ It can adapt to various types and speeds of trains. Because the moving block system basically overcomes the problem of the information jump of trackside to on-board equipment of the quasi-moving block and fixed block system, which improves the stability of the train operation and increases the comfort of passengers.

⑤ It can realize energy saving control, optimize train operation statistics processing, shorten operation time and other multi-objective control.

⑥ The moving block system, especially the system which adopts high-speed data transmission mode, will bring the value-added of information utilization and function expansion, which is beneficial to the improvement of modernization level.

⑦ The new concept of "signal through communication" should be established so that the train and the trackside can be closely integrated and processed as a whole, so as to change the isolation of the former onboard and trackside equipment, and on-board based status. This means that with the uniform standard protocol, it is possible to realize the interconnection of different types of trains between different lines. For the signal system, the so-called connected connection operation mainly refers to that the ground equipment of one system can be connected with the ground equipment of another system, the on-board equipment of the system can work together with the ground equipment of another system, and the on-board equipment of different manufacturers at the head and tail of the same train can implement the train operation control on the same line.

⑧ Because of the high requirements of real-time and responsiveness, moving blocking systems require higher requirements for system integrity than other forms of blocking, and the reliability of the system should also have higher requirements.

⑨ The reliability and safety of system transmission is the core of system concern, especially the use of free space wave transmission information of the moving block system based on wireless has higher reliability and safety requirements.

CBTC has two main categories: based on cable between rails and wireless communication.

A. CBTC based on cable between rails.

This kind of ATC system is mainly composed of control center equipment, transmission cable between rails and on-board equipment, as shown in figure 2.25.

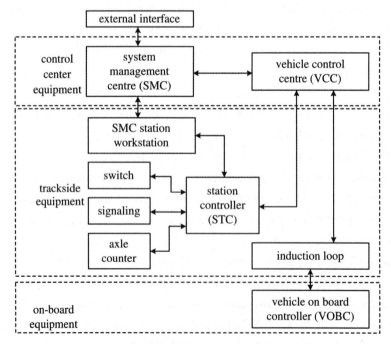

Figure 2.25 CBTC based on cable between rails

The connection of indoor and outdoor equipment of the ATC based on cable between rails is realized by two-level control method, that is the control center is connected with several repeater sets along the line. A repeater can connect up to 128 cable loops, The information exchange between the control center and cable laying between the rails will carry out intermediate transformation (frequency transformation, level transformation, power amplification, etc.) in the repeater.

In this kind of continuous overspeed protection system, the cable between rails is the only information channel between vehicle on-board and trackside equipment. In order to resist the interference of traction current and realize train positioning, the cable between the rails should cross at regular intervals (for example, every 25 m).

B. CBTC based on wireless communication.

The system structure of the typical wireless moving block system is shown in figure 2.26. The system takes the train as the center, and its main subsystems include: zone controller, vehicle on board controller, automatic train supervision (central control), data communication system and train operator display, etc.

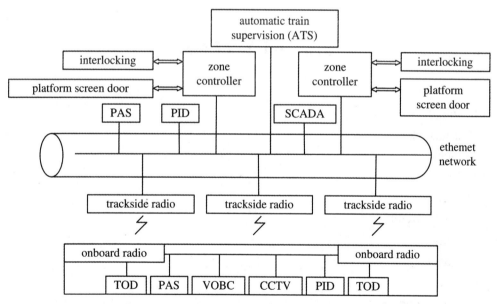

Figure 2.26 The system structure of the typical wireless moving block system
(CCTV-closed circuit television, PAS-public address system, PID-passenger information display, SCADA-supervisory control and data acquisition, TOD-train operator display, VOBC-vehicle on board control)

The zone controller (ZC) is the local computer of the zone and corresponds to the interlocking area. It maintains the safety information communication of all trains in the control zone through the data communication system. ZC tracks the train according to the location report from the train and releases the movement authority (MA) for the train in the zone to implement interlocking. The zone controller adopts the test redundancy configuration of two-out of three.

ATS with redundant structure can communicate with all train control subsystems for transmission command and supervisory subsystem status.

Vehicle on-board controller (COBV) corresponds to the train, realizing the function of ATP and ATO. The vehicle on-board controller also adopts the redundant configuration of two-out of three. The train is located by the on-board balise transponder, antenna and the balise (beacon) on the ground. The speed generator is used for speed measurement and calibration of train location.

The train operator display (TOD) provides the interface between the driver and VOBC and ATS, The information displayed includes maximum allowable speed, current measurement speed, distance to station, train operation mode and system error information, etc.

The channel of the data communication system can be free of radio wave, waveguide or leakage cable.

2.6 KEY TERMS

(1) signal
(2) interlock
(3) block
(4) route
(5) switch
(6) track circuit
(7) relay
(8) wheel
(9) axle
(10) axle counter
(11) switch machine
(12) manual block
(13) semi-automatic block
(14) automatic block
(15) fixed block
(16) moving block
(17) communication based train control (CBTC)
(18) three-aspect automatic block

(19) four-aspect automatic block
(20) relay interlocking
(21) computer based interlocking (CBI)
(22) human-machine interface (HMI)
(23) automatic train control (ATC)
(24) automatic train protection (ATP)
(25) automatic train operation (ATO)
(26) automatic train supervision (ATS)
(27) beacon
(28) balise
(29) vehicle control centre (VCC)
(30) vehicle on board controller (VOBC)
(31) zone controller (ZC)
(32) movement authority (MA)
(33) 3C technology: computer technology, communication technology and control technology
(34) closed circuit television (CCTV)
(35) public address system (PAS)
(36) passenger information display (PID)
(37) supervisory control and data acquisition (SCADA)
(38) train operator display (TOD)
(39) vehicle on-board controller (COBV)

2.7 EXERCISES

Ⅰ Match the terms with correct definitions or explanations.

| automatic signal   block signal   fixed signal |
| automatic train operation (ATO)   automatic train protection (ATP) |
| automatic train supervision (ATS) |

1. A signal that is controlled automatically by certain conditions of the track section that it protects.   (   )

2. In rail operations, a signal at a fixed location that indicates a condition that affects the movement of a train.   (   )

3. A fixed signal installed at the entrance of a block to govern trains entering and using that section of track, cab-see control system, cab signal.   (   )

4. The subsystem within automatic train control that provides fail-safe protection against collisions, excessive speed, and other hazardous conditions.   (   )

5. The subsystem within automatic train control that monitors trains, adjusts the performance of individual trains to maintain schedules, and provides data for adjusting service to minimize the inconveniences otherwise caused by irregularities.   (   )

6. The subsystem within automatic train control that performs such functions as speed control, programmed stopping, and (sometimes) door operation.   (   )

Ⅱ Answer the following questions according to the text.
1. Describe the importance of signaling system.

2. Introduction the advantages of moving block.

3. What are the functions of computer interlocking?

4. Briefly describe the characteristics and structure of CBTC.

Chapter 3　Operation & Management

> The purpose of the train operating plan is to provide the necessary information for the E & M and operation and management plans, based on the traffic demand forecast, route alignment, and performance of rolling stock. The following information should be provided:
> The minimum headway;
> The running time between terminals and the required number of rolling stock;
> The annual train-kilometers and the annual working volume data required for the operation & maintenance plan.

3.1　Station Operation

3.1.1　Classification of Stations

Stations are classified into terminal stations, intermediate stations, junction stations, and connecting stations, as shown in figure 3.1.

(1) Terminal station: this generally refers to stations at the end of lines, but includes stations in the middle of networks where most trains terminate their journeys, as shown in figure 3.2.

① Pass-through type: stations through which trains can pass.

② Heading type: stations where all trains come to a stop in terms of route.

(2) Intermediate station: intermediate stations on route networks. Most stations fall under this heading.

(3) Junction station: stations where different lines break off from an intermediate stop on a different line.

(4) Connecting station: stations where stations on two lines are adjoining or intersect on differing levels.

① Stations where two lines are joined in close proximity are known as connecting stations.

② Stations where two lines cross on different levels are known as intersection stations.

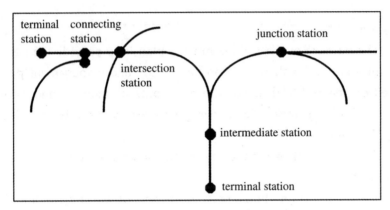

Figure 3.1 Classification of stations

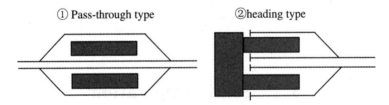

Figure 3.2 Classification of terminal stations

Stations are divided into island platform or separate platform, and the features of each are given below (table 3.1).

Table 3.1 Types of platform

	island platform	separate platform
Advantage	Generally, total platform width will be minimized with same furnishings because passengers bound for both directions will share a single escalator. Also, it will be easier for passengers to select the platform.	It will involve simple straight track arrangement. It will involve less passenger congestion, even if trains in both directions arrive at the same time.
Disadvantage	It will require expansion of the distance between the main lines.	Twice the number of escalators and/or elevators will be required compared to the island type.

Track Layout

The following will be the main requirements for the track layout:

Starting station has to have shuttling facilities, namely: turnouts, head shunting line, etc. If it is possible, the final station has to be arranged in four lines and double platforms, owing to the need to connect to the workshop/depot behind the station, as shown in figure 3.3. Such an arrangement will also be beneficial for the future operation and extension of the route. Head shunting lines are required at intervals of approximately 5 km to provide for emergency operations and/or for the maintenance of permanent way.

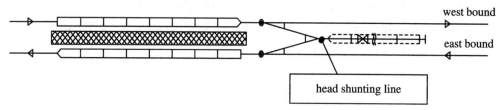

Figure 3.3 Track layout for starting station

From the viewpoint of the operation plan, it is proposed to locate two Y-shaped tracks at Stations No. 5 and No. 9. These tracks will be used for temporary parking of troubled trains, and/or shunting of maintenance rolling stock, emergency shuttling, etc.

Typical stations have simple straight tracks and an island platform without switches and/or crossings, as shown in figure 3.4. Therefore, they are not cri-tical points for alignment planning.

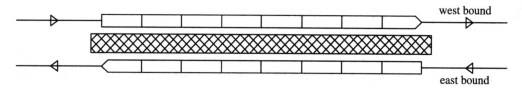

Figure 3.4 Track layout for typical station

This station is the terminal station for phase 1 and the connecting station with the workshop/depot line, as shown in figure 3.5. Thus, it needs some function for shuttling and shunting to the depot. Therefore, it is desirable to arrange two platforms and four tracks at this location. The track layout will be designed such that all tracks can access each direction, as shown in figure 3.5. Conversely, the design of the track layout will allow all trains coming from either direction to arrive at every platform.

Leading Line to Workshop/Depot

There is a difference of more than 10 m between the track level of Station No. 15 and that of the Workshop/Depot (W/D). Trains entering the workshops will have to reverse from the end of the line at Station No. 15.

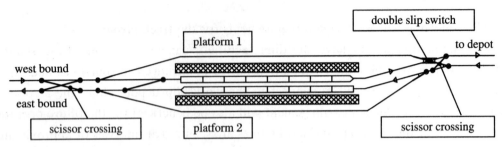

Figure 3.5 Track layout for terminal station

The proposed lead track layout which will allow this operation is as shown in figure 3.6. This alignment is planned to position the lead line between the two mainlines in order to avoid a level crossing on the mainline.

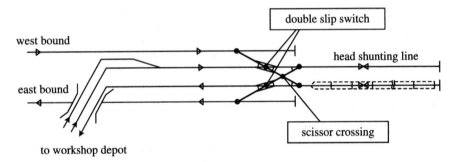

Figure 3.6 Track layout for workshop/depot leading track layout

3.1.2 Platform Screen Doors

Platform screen doors (PSDs) and platform edge doors (PEDs) at train or subway stations screen the platform from the train. They are a relatively new addition to many metro systems around the world, some having been retrofitted to established systems. They are widely used in Asian and European metro systems.

(1) Door Types

Although the terms are often used interchangeably, platform screen doors are full height, total barriers between the station floor and ceiling, while platform edge doors are full height but do not reach the ceiling and thus do not create a total barrier.

(2) Platform Screen Doors

These doors help to:

- Prevent accidental falls off the platform onto the lower track area, suicide attempts and homicides by pushing.

- Prevent or reduce wind felt by the passengers caused by the piston effect which could in some circumstances make people fall over.
- Reduce the risk of accidents, especially from service trains passing through the station at high speeds.
- Improve climate control within the station (heating, ventilation, and air conditioning are more effective when the station is physically isolated from the tunnel).
- Improve security — access to the tracks and tunnels is restricted.
- Lower costs — eliminate the need for motor menor conductors when used in conjunction with Automatic Train Operation, thereby reducing manpower costs.
- Prevent litter build up on the track, which can be a fire risk.
- Improve the sound quality of platform announcements, as background noise from the tunnels and trains that are entering or exiting is reduced.

Their primary disadvantage is their cost; installing a system typically costs several million USD per station. When used to retrofit older systems, they limit the kind of rolling stock that may be used on a line, as train doors must have exactly the same spacing as the platform doors; this results in additional costs due to depot upgrades and otherwise unnecessary purchases of rolling stock.

The doors also pose their own safety risks. The primary risk is that people may be trapped between the platform doors and the train carriage, and be subsequently crushed when the train begins to move. Cases of this happening are rare, and may depend upon door design.

(3) Automatic Platform Gate

Automatic platform gates (or platform edge doors or half-height platform screen doors as referred to by some manufacturers) are chest-height sliding doors at the edge of railway platforms to prevent passengers from falling off the platform edge onto the railway tracks. Like full-height platform screen doors (figure 3.7), these platform gates slide open or closed simultaneously with the train doors.

Half-height platform gates (figure 3.8) are cheaper to install than platform screen doors, which require more metallic framework for support. Some railway operators may therefore prefer such an option to improve safety at railway platforms and, at the same time, keep costs low and non-air-conditioned platforms naturally ventilated.

However, these gates are less effective than full platform screen doors in preventing people from intentionally jumping onto the tracks.

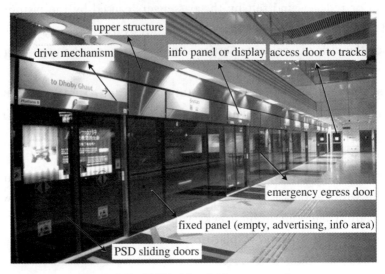

Figure 3.7 Full-height platform screen doors

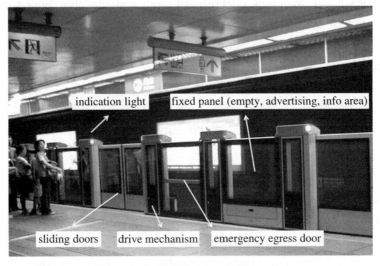

Figure 3.8 Half-height platform gates

3.1.3 Automated Fare Collection (AFC) System

Mass rapid transit system handles large number of passengers. Ticket issue and fare collection play a vital role in the efficient and proper operation of the system. To achieve this objective, ticketing system shall be simple, easy to use/operate, easy on accounting facilities, capable of issuing single/multiple journey tickets, amenable for quick fare changes and require overall lesser manpower. Automatic fare collection system meets these requirements. Fare collection technology development is as shown in figure 3.9 below.

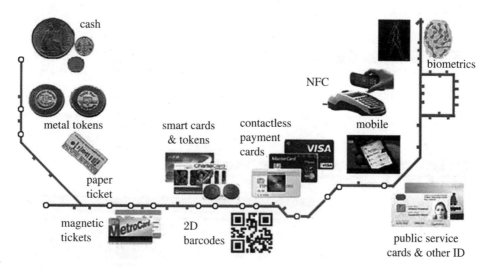

Figure 3.9 Fare collection technology development

(1) Proposed Automatic Fare Collection System

Keeping in view metro railways automatic fare collection system and the fact that contactless card/ token technology proves to be cheaper than other technologies in life cycle cost due to reduced maintenance as it has less wear and tear and is less prone to dusty environment, it is proposed to provide computer based automatic fare collection system with contactless smart token/card type ticketing for the varanasi MRTS.

The equipments for the same may be provided at each station viz. Automatic fare gates, ticket office machines, ticket readers, portable ticket decoders, central and station computers, passenger operated machines/ticket vending machines (POMs/TVMs) and UPS. The typical AFC system operation process and architecture is shown in figure 3.10 and figure 3.11 respectively.

The AFC system shall be interoperable with AFC systems to be planned in future. The AFC system shall also have functionality of interface to CCHS (central clearing house system) facility including CCHS hardware and software with provision of integration with other transit (metro, bus etc.) and non-transit (parking, toll etc.) which may be planned in future in line with the state / national policy.

In addition, the proposed AFC system shall also be NFC (near field communication) enabled so that customers can use their NFC enabled mobile phones for metro travel.

Facility of recharging of travel cards using cash, debit/credit cards and net banking/ web portal shall also be available. AFC system shall also support offsite sales terminals also, wherein cards and tokens can be dispensed at locations outside metro premises.

(2) Ticket Types

There are two main types of tickets used in AFC systems-the single journey ticket

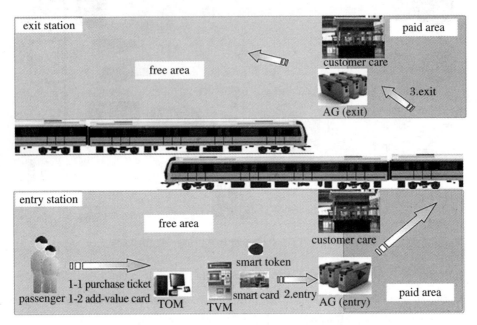

Figure 3.10 AFC system operation process

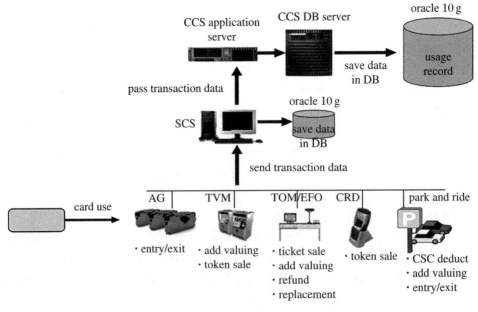

Figure 3.11 AFC system architecture

and the stored value ticket. Smart card, recently introduced for some mass transit systems, is an entering form of stored value ticket. The single journey ticket is essential for the occasional traveller or visitor to the system. The ticket is good for one journey. Normally, the ticket is inserted into the entering fare gate and the gate released if valid, the same ticket is used to exit the destination station but it will be retained by the exit gate.

It is becoming the practice on many systems, to restrict the sales of single journey tickets to TVMs. If passengers ask for a single journey ticket at the ticket office, they will be directed to use the TVM. Change may or may not be offered according to the policy of the operator. In Bangkok, the new metro system has to employ extra staff to give change for TVMs at busy times.

- Single tickets.

The fare structure for paper single tickets was simplified in January 2006. Fares for single paper tickets have been set deliberately high in order to encourage users to use either travel cards or oyster pre-pay fares, which are substantially lower (by up to £2.50 per journey) than paper tickets.

Return tickets are sold at twice the price of a single ticket. A travel card is often cheaper than a return ticket and will automatically be provided by ticket machines and ticket office staff.

- Travel card.

Daily, seven-day, monthly and annual travel cards are also available, allowing unlimited rides in two or more zones on the London Underground and most other forms of public transport in London, including most National Rail services, buses, Tramlink and Docklands Light Railway, but not the Emirates Air Line (cable car) cross-Thames service. Travel cards are also available for "odd periods" of between one month and a year at some retailers. Most regular travellers use travel cards, and they are usually better value for money than single tickets for anyone making multiple daily journeys or using multiple forms of public transport (train/tube, tube/bus, etc.). Any period travel card is valid at any time of day, any day of the week.

Day travel cards are valid at any time on any day, although they are usually only sold Monday — Friday before 9:30 am, while cheaper off-peak travel cards are only valid for use on trains & London Underground services after 9:30 am on weekdays (excluding bank holidays) but any time on weekends & holidays. News agents and other designated "Ticket Stop" shops can no longer sell any form of paper tickets and now only offer oyster facilities; one day paper bus passes can be obtained from ticket vending machines at some bus stops in central London. Both peak and off-peak day travel cards are valid on all journeys started before 4:30 on the day after the date of issue.

- Oyster card.

In 2003, transport for London launched the oyster card. It is a proximity card, which on buses, trams and on the underground allows a traveller to touch the card on one of the yellow readers positioned on the automatic entrance and exit faregates rather than feeding it through a card ticket reader.

Unlike card tickets, the oyster card is not disposable, and value — either "pay as you go" balance or Travel cards — can be added to it at computerised ticket machines and at ticket offices. Where pay as you go credit is used, the cost of each journey is deducted from a stored balance. As of October 2005, weekly, monthly and annual travel cards issued by London Underground or directly by transport for London are only available on oyster cards.

The fare structure is now designed to encourage the use of oyster cards. Daily travel cards are not available on oyster, but a system called "capping" ensures that on each day of use no more than the equivalent travel card price is deducted. Prior to January 2010 the oyster cap was 50p less than a travel card, but now the cap for oyster and travel card is the same. The balance can be automatically topped up with funds from a credit or debit card when the balance becomes low, a feature known as "auto top-up". Tickets and pay as you go credit can be purchased via a website or over the telephone.

The oyster card system is designed to eliminate the need to purchase tickets at the station for most users. Following the implementation of the technology London underground reduced the number of staff working in ticket offices.

- Contactless.

Contactless Visa, Maestro, MasterCard and American Express debit and credit bank cards, as well as contactless enabled smart phones and smart watches using Apple Pay and Android Pay are accepted for travel on London Underground, London Overground, Docklands Light Rail, most National Rail, London Tramlink and bus services.

Operation of the system is exactly the same as the oyster smartcard; customers should touch their card on the validation devices (entry/exit gates, passenger validators) at the start and again at the end of their journey to ensure the correct fare is paid. Only adult, non-discount, "Pay As You Go" fares are available with contactless payment cards. Travel cards may not be loaded onto a contactless payment card as they may be with oyster.

Unlike Pay As You Go on oyster (where the stored value held on the card is adjusted as the passenger touches their card as they enter/exit stations or board buses), transactions made with contactless payment cards are processed by a central processing system. The total charge of all travel accrued throughout a day is settled overnight, meaning that a customer will see one transaction for each day in which they have travelled on their credit card or bank statement. Daily travel charges are settled directly against the customer's debit or credit card account; no "topping up" is required.

Like oyster, contactless implements daily capping, whereby the customer pays no more than the price of an equivalent daily travel card. Unlike oyster, contactless also offers "Monday — Sunday Capping", whereby the combination of products that gives the "best value" is selected (from a range of single fares, extension fares, daily and weekly travel cards) to ensure that the customer never pays more than is necessary for their travel. The customer does not have to know their travel plans in advance. Monday — Sunday Capping is distinct from an oyster 7-day travel card in that the latter may be purchased on any day of the week, whereas Monday-Sunday Capping "lapses" at the start of the travel day on Monday.

- Faregates.

The purpose of an AFC system is to ensure that every passenger has a valid ticket when he enters the railway and that he pays the correct fare for the journey he has made. The most effective way of doing this is to impose a barrier of faregates across the station entrance which will only allow passengers with valid tickets to enter the system and board a train.

One example of how design has evolved is in the new slim line faregates designed for the Jubilee Line extension in London. The gate flaps are designed to prevent passengers from climbing over them or crawling under them. In Hong Kong, older faregates introduced with the opening of the first part of the system in 1979 are of the tripod variety. They have been modified to take the Octopus smart card as well as the original plastic single journey tickets. The smart card does not need to pass through the reader. It can be read electronically as long as the card is within 100 mm of the reader.

3.1.4 Station Opening and Closing Procedures

Rail transit system stations and the personnel who work in them set the stage for customers' transit experiences. The service and treatment customers receive in stations are influential in developing customer loyalty. Station personnel should strive to relate to customers in a helpful and pleasant manner. It is also important for station personnel to be alert and vigilant for suspicious or unusual activity and behavior and to report unusual behavior through prescribed methods. Customer relations for station personnel involves a broad range of activities including, but not limited to, interactions between station personnel and customers; provision of travel information; provision of service to customers with disabilities; public address announcements; and responses to emergency situations. Station personnel are often involved in practices to ensure revenue procedures are adhered to and that problems arising from these transactions are properly resolved.

Training should be provided for station personnel in the methods and procedures of opening and closing stations.

(1) Station Opening Checklist

A specific checklist should be developed that identifies the elements and procedures that station personnel are to follow when opening their stations. The elements on this checklist may include the following:

- Check in with designated authority.
- Inspect station and immediate surroundings for safety and security haza-rds and problems or weather related issues.
- Operate escalator and elevator controls and features.
- Ensure that fare equipment is operable and secure.
- Ensure that communication equipment is operable (e.g., platform telephones and TDD features, public address system, radio check with operation control center, etc.).
- Activate other systems in station, such as closed-circuit television monitors.
- Inventory booth/kiosk for necessary supplies and equipment and review station logs and bulletins/notices.
- Inventory and stock travel information brochures.
- Open security gates/doors to open station for service.
- Update station elevator status boards.

(2) Station Closing Checklist

Prior to closing their stations, station personnel must inspect them for unusual conditions and ensure that all customers have exited after the last revenue train has departed the station.

During this station-closing activity, it is presumed that station personnel will be expected to follow many of the same procedures and/or elements as specified for station openings when similar situations exist unless the RTA defines otherwise. Elements and tasks that a rail transit system may include in its station-closing checklist include the following:

- Empty bins/discard debris and garbage.
- Check that all equipment is operational and secure (e.g., the revenue equipment, elevators and escalators are working properly and then turned off).
- Check that the track, stairs, elevators, escalators, ramps, floors, platforms, etc., are free of hazards and repugnant or disagreeable conditions.
- Ensure that booth/kiosk equipment is secure.
- Check out according to procedures with appropriate authorities.
- Secure the booth/kiosk door.
- Activate the station alarm if available.
- Close station gates/grilles.

- Exit station and lock station doors.
- Verify that no passengers are present in the station.

(3) **Definitions**

Customer relations: The practices that a rail transit system employs to interact with customers.

Emergency: An unexpected event related to the operation of passenger train service involving significant threat to the health or safety of one or more persons, requiring immediate action. Examples include: derailment, highway/rail grade crossing accident, passenger or employee fatality or serious illness/injury, evacuation of train or security situation.

Rail transit agency: Any entity that provides services on a rail fixed guideway public transportation system.

Hazard: Any real or potential condition that can cause injury, death, or damage or loss of equipment or property.

Control center/central control/operations control center: The facility where rail operations such as train control, train dispatching, train supervision and related field activities are accomplished for the entire rail transit system or for specific segments of a system if there is more than one such facility.

3.1.5 Passenger Service

P: Passenger   M: Metro staff

Dialogue 1 (line information)
P: Excuse me. Is this train bound for Railway Station?
M: Yes, you can take Line 2 for Railway Station, please follow the guidance to take the train.
P: How can I get there?
M: You can take Line 2 towards Airport Station, it's 3 stations away from here.

Dialogue 2 (line information)
P: I would like to go to Central Hospital Station, but I don't know how to get there.
M: The Central Hospital Station is on Line 1, you can take Line 2 and then transfer Line 1 at the Railway Station.
P: How many stations does it take?
M: It's 3 stations away from here.

Dialogue 3 (train schedule)
P: Excuse me. When does the last train/first train leave for Zoo Station?
M: The first/last train leaves at 6:02/22:32.
P: How long does it take to get there?

M: It takes about 10 minutes.

Dialogue 4 (station exit)

P: Excuse me. When does the first train leave for Railway Station?
M: The first train leaves at 6:02.
P: My train departure time is 6:45, can I catch the train?
M: The Zoo Station is 5 stations from Railway Station, each station takes 2 minutes to travel, you can/can't catch the train if you take the first train.

Dialogue 5 (station exit)

P: Excuse me. Where is the nearest bus stop?
M: Leave the station from Exit A.
P: Is there an escalator at Exit A?
M: Yes, there is an escalator at Exit A. Let me help you to carry the luggage to A.

Dialogue 6 (ticketing)

P: Excuse me, I put the ticket into the slot but it was returned.
M: Would you please let me check your ticket? ... You come from Luohu Station and the fee should be 3 yuan but the balance of your token is 2 yuan. Please give 1 yuan more here.
P: I see. Here you are.

Dialogue 7 (TVM out of service)

M: Good morning. Can I help you?
P: Good morning. What's wrong with this machine?
M: This TVM is out of service. Please go to another one to buy a single ticket.
P: I can't buy one all the same. Why doesn't it take my money?
M: Sorry. Our machine only accepts 5 yuan notes, half yuan coins or 1 yuan coins.
P: But I don't have these kinds of money. What shall I do?
M: You can exchange at the ticket booth over there.
P: Oh, I see. Thank you!

Dialogue 8 (AG out of service)

P: Excuse me, I put my single ticket into the slot just now but the door did not open.
M: I am sorry. Can you point out the gate?
P: (Pointing out) This one over there.
M: Oh, I got it. Please sign your name in this form and I'll give you a free ticket to get out.

3.2 Train Operation

3.2.1 Terminal Types

In rail transit systems, there are three main types of terminals: stub-end, relay, and loop terminals. They represent three different ways trains can be turned at a terminal. This section describes the layout and the path of train movement for each terminal type.

(1) Stub-end Terminal

The stub-end terminal is probably the most common type of rail transit terminal in the US. In a stub-end terminal, trains arrive and depart from the same platform and so all the passenger and crew activities happen during the time the train stays on the platform. Figure 3.12 shows the typical train movement at a 2-track stub-end terminal. Depending upon availability, trains can berth at either platform at the terminal. Usually the platform that is aligned with the departure track is preferred so that the departing train will not interfere with any incoming train on the arrival track.

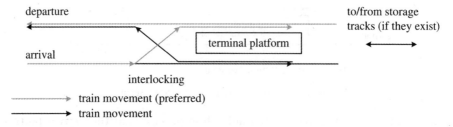

Figure 3.12 Train movement in a stub-end terminal

Under low frequency operations, only 1 platform (the preferred) may be used for train turnback. In high frequency operations, both platforms would be needed for train processing. In this case trains would enter the terminal alternating on either side of the platform, and then process passengers and wait there for their next departure.

Conflicting train movement at the crossover in front of the terminal will occur, resulting in delays to some trains. If a train yard is located behind the terminal, pullouts and layups can occur at either track.

Note that besides the 2-track stub-end terminal, there are stub-end terminals with three tracks at the terminal; one way to configure a 3-track stub-end terminal is illustrated in figure 3.13. Similar to a 2-track stub-end terminal, trains berth at one of the three platforms according to availability and priority. Usually the third track is used for pullouts and layups, whereas the remaining tracks will be used for ordinary turnbacks.

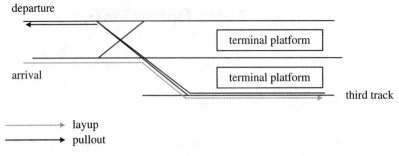

Figure 3.13 Layout of a 3-track stub-end terminal

A 3-track stub-end terminal is preferred to a 2-track stub-end because the extra track allows more flexibility in operations. For example, when there is a problem train that requires inspection at terminal, it can be diverted to the third track; while ordinary trains can continue their turnbacks on the two remaining tracks. Also, having an extra track allows pullouts and layups without interfering with ordinary turnback movements.

(2) Relay Terminal

In a relay terminal, trains use separate tracks/platforms for arrival and departure. Figure 3.14 shows the layout of a 2-track relay terminal.

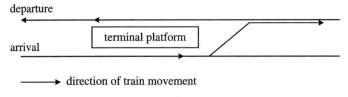

Figure 3.14 Train movement in a relay terminal

Upon completion of the arrival and unloading processes at the arrival platform, the train will proceed behind the terminal, then the crew (operator or platform crew) changes ends and resets the train control, and then drives the train back to the departure platform for passenger boarding and to await its next departure.

The relay terminal has a higher crew cost then does a stub-end terminal, since the crew is needed to operate the train beyond the terminal during the turnback. If a train yard is located at the terminal, layups will go through the arrival platform before entering the yard, and pullouts would enter the departure track before starting revenue service.

(3) Loop Terminal

Similar to a relay terminal, trains move behind the terminal to reverse directions. After depositing passengers at the arrival platform, the train proceeds through a loop track behind the terminal to the departure platform where it loads passengers and awaits

its next departure, as shown in figure 3.15.

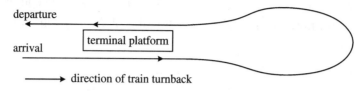

Figure 3.15 Train movement in a loop terminal

A loop terminal can allow a faster turn back of train then a relay terminal, as crews do not have to change ends beyond the terminal. However, loop terminals require more land for the loop track and the train movement distance is generally larger than for relay operations.

3.2.2 Train Service Planning

(1) Train Operation Headway

This is the name given to the elapsed time between trains passing a fixed point in the same direction over the same track. It is usually expressed in seconds or minutes e.g. "trains were running at a 4-minute headway". Another way of expressing it is as trains per hour (tph).

A well run railway will conduct research to determine how many fare paying customers are likely to show up at various times of the day and will operate their trains to suit. In many instances the patronage numbers will show that it is possible to run trains at even intervals or at a given "headway". This may be at two hours for a long distance, main line route or two minutes for a metro.

Once established, the headway is used in calculating the number of trains required for a particular service, the train performance requirements and signalling requirements.

(2) Round Trip Time

Once the patronage is determined, the train service has to be planned to carry the people who turn up. During the peak hours, this can be a lot of people. The frequency and number of trains required has to be calculated to match. First the run times are worked out, again by a computer program which includes the profile of the line (curves, gradients, station locations, dwell times at stations etc.) and the performance of the trains to be used. On heavily used lines, the program may incorporate the patronage figures to estimate the number of seconds each train has to stand or "dwell" at each station while loading and unloading takes place.

The diagram of our imaginary Forest line above (figure 3.16) shows in red the computer generated arrival times, in seconds, for a train running in each direction. Added together and with allowances for terminal standing times, the program will eventually provide a "round trip time", i.e., the time it takes to run from one end of the line to the other, wait at the terminus, run back to the starting place and wait for the next round trip departure time.

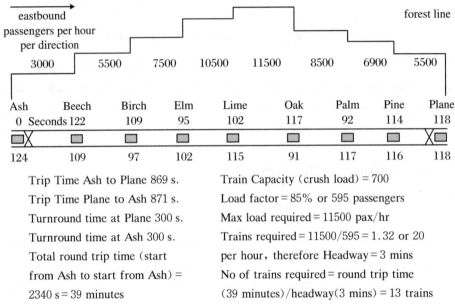

Figure 3.16 Train service planning

In our example above, the run time from Ash to Plane is 869 seconds and the time back from Plane to Ash is 871 seconds. There is a 300 second dwell at each terminus to allow the train to change direction and load/unload passengers. This is actually longer than needed but we usually leave in a bit of extra time for delays — known as "recovery time". This time is also used to give a round trip time to balance the service interval. The end result — our round trip time — is 39 minutes.

3.2.3 Audible and Hand Signals

These signals shall apply consistently to employees working in the yard and/or maintenance facility. As a minimum, the following audible and hand signals shall be considered:

• Audible signals:

Alert for people on the track.

Acknowledgement or answer to any signal not otherwise provided.

Call for signals (request for directions).

Stand clear, the train is about to move.

• Hand signals:

Stop or remain standing.

Reduce speed.

Proceed.

Back up.

- Radio protocols:

Use of radio communications to govern decision to move (where applicable).

- Hand signals must be given:

Facing the Rail Traffic.

In such a position that there can be no misunderstanding as to the purpose of the Hand signals.

In a clear and timely manner; and so that the hand signals will be received and acted upon only by those who are being signalled.

During Shunting Operations, where it is not possible to face the Rail Traffic, the Hand signaller must be satisfied that the Rail Traffic Crew can see all hand signals or use an alternative method of communications (e.g. radio).

- A hand signaller must:

Be in or have access to a Safe Place;

Be in clear view of those who are being signalled; and as required, communicate with: train controllers; protection officers (PO); and rail traffic crew.

If conditions such as visibility change, the hand signaller must tell the PO.

When hand signalling at a level crossing or controlled absolute signal and visibility changes, the hand signaller must tell the train controller.

In the electrified area, hand signals conveyed by hand, flag or light must not be given above the head unless the worker giving the hand signal is standing on the ground. Table 3.2 shows the general hand signals below.

Table 3.2 General hand signals

Hand signal/ Instruction	Verbal command	Using flags	Using lights	Using hands
Stop	"STOP" or "red light" during Shunting Operations only	Steady red flag	Steady red light	Both hands held high

Continued

Hand signal/ Instruction	Verbal command	Using flags	Using lights	Using hands
Emergency or danger	"STOP, STOP, STOP"	Vigorous and erratic waving of flag	Waving any light in a vigorous and erratic manner	Vigorous and erratic waving of arms
Warning/caution	"Reduce to, and travel at restricted speed"	Wave yellow flag slowly	Wave yellow light slowly	Nil
Proceed at normal speed	"Proceed at Normal speed"	Steady green flag	Steady green light	Nil
All clear	"I am aware of your approach" "clear to proceed"	Nil	Steady white light	One hand held up

3.3 Safe Operations Requirements

"Safe operations" is a term that defines and encompasses all activities necessary for the safe movement of trains and OTE. Safe operations require all employees to be familiar with and comply with the rules and procedures that govern the movement of trains and OTE in yards and maintenance facilities. Communication between RTS staff members of different departments (as required) operating within the yard and maintenance facility is a key component of safe operations and helps ensure coordination among all

personnel. Safe operations may also encompass other elements, such as:
- Performing inspection, as defined by the RTS, prior to moving train within the yard or maintenance facility.
- Conducting a pre-trip/departure inspection (e.g. minimum operating standards equipment list) prior to entering the main line.
- Operating trains at safe speeds.
- Checking switches for proper alignment.
- Performing safety stops.

Safe operations mandate that employees perform their respective duties in a safe manner while using proper safeguards and with a general understanding of how their actions may affect others.

3.3.1 Yard and Maintenance Facility

The RTS shall develop and implement rules and procedures and/or develop and include a specific element within its roadway worker protection (RWP) program that specifically governs the actions of employees while performing their duties in yards and maintenance facilities. These rules and procedures shall be appropriate for the RTS, taking into consideration safe practices involving:
- Operating environment.
- Types of equipment used in the yard (e.g. trains and OTE).
- Equipment and tools used.
- Infrastructure.
- Safe train and OTE operating speed.
- Geographical location.
- Track, switches, traction power, and signals.
- Climatic conditions.
- Layout of the yard and maintenance facility.

The RTS's procedures shall also describe specific safety precautions for train operators, OTE operators, and maintenance workers while performing safety-sensitive duties, as well as other individuals in the yard. The RTS shall identify safety precautions associated with energized third rails, energized overhead wires, fueling facilities, and/or train and OTE movement.

The RTS shall develop procedures for ensuring that all trains and OTE are safe and are ready for service.

Typically, this includes an appropriate physical inspection of the train or OTE.

(1) Movement Authorization

The RTS shall establish rules and/or procedures for the authorization of train and

OTE movements within yards and maintenance facilities, as well as movements into and out of yards and maintenance facilities. The level of control required will be determined by the size, complexity and operating practices of the RTS.

Train and OTE movement authorization must be clearly defined and permission granted by operating rules and/or procedures, operations control center, vehicle maintenance management, or from a yard supervisor.

Train movements in the yard may also be controlled by signal, or trains may be operated by line of sight. In the absence of signal protection, the RTS shall develop specific operating procedures to ensure a safe operating environment in the yard.

(2) Track Classification

The RTS shall identify all tracks according to their operating classification. This may include categories such as main tracks, running tracks, side tracks, test tracks, storage tracks, yard tracks, maintenance tracks or some other designation appropriate to that particular RTS. The RTS shall also designate the yard limit, determine how yard tracks can be used, and manage yard track access.

(3) Securement of Trains and OTE

The RTS shall establish rules and/or procedures for the safe, proper securement of trains and OTE from unintended movement and work to ensure that tracks, trains, equipment, and facilities in the yard are secure and access to these assets is limited.

As determined by the RTS, employees operating trains or OTE in yards are responsible for knowing and practicing the safe and proper securement of a trains or OTE from unintended movement at the completion of a move.

The RTS shall establish a procedure to prevent the movement of a vehicle while individuals are working on or around the vehicle or for other specific requirements. The RTS may consider the use of flag or illuminated light protection of equipment, chocks, derailers, or other methods of protection.

(4) Train and OTE Inspection and Operation

The RTS shall require any employee operating a train or OTE to visually check all cars of the train or the OTE and identify any defects or restrictions to movement that may impact safe operation before movement. The RTS shall require the employee operating the train or OTE to perform all operational tests required by the RTS in the prescribed manner to verify that the train or OTE is capable of safely operating before movement. The employee operating the train or OTE shall sound an audible warning prior to movement in order to warn personnel of train or OTE movement. When coupling or uncoupling cars, the train operator shall understand and comply with RTS coupling and uncoupling procedures, which may or may not be different from mainline tracks and shall properly secure all cars being added or cut from the train.

Before moving a train, the operator shall ensure that the train has the correct number of cars assigned.

(5) Safety Stops

Safety stops are required in advance of a RTS defined must-stop situation. Where yard moves are controlled by the train operator, the route of an assigned move shall not be changed without positive communications with other train operators, OTE operators, yard supervisors, and any other employee who supervises train movements in the yard.

3.3.2 Movement of Trains

The RTS shall establish procedures for moving trains into and out of maintenance facilities. Where applicable, the RTS shall, at a minimum, address the following:
- Clear identifications of who can authorize train movement into and out of the maintenance facility.
- Requirements to clearly communicate train moves into and out of the maintenance facility, including use of "safety stops" prior to entering and exiting the facility.
- Maximum allowable speeds inside the maintenance facility.
- Flagging requirements, to include who is authorized to flag a train into or out of a maintenance facility.
- Requirements to respond to and follow various hand signals.
- Train operator instructions and requirements on following fixed signals inside the maintenance facility, if equipped.
- Requirements to fully open and secure maintenance facility doors.
- Safe vehicle operations within the maintenance facility.
- Inspections prior to moving a train or OTE shall include.
  — Clear areas around tracks — adjacent facility structures, portable equipment, vehicle doors and panels, etc.
  — Review under (pits) and above (catwalk, cranes, etc.) train for clearance.
- Requirements to be aware of any train or OTE defects that could affect the safe operation of the train or OTE prior to moving the train or OTE.
- Requirements to ensure that propulsion power is available inside the maintenance facility to make the desired move.
- Precautions to take to prevent inadvertent and unintended energization of overhead wires or the third rail by bridging two sections of a power distribution system with a train.
- Precautions to take to ensure train has a clear path to its destination prior to flagging a train inside the maintenance facility.

- Safety requirements for all personnel involved in the movement of trains and on track equipment or those within the safety envelope.
- Requirements for the proper securement of trains or OTE at the completion of movement.
- Prohibitions of reverse movements, as applicable.
- Requirements for proper use of portable traction power systems (e. g. bugging railcars into and out of a maintenance facility).

Definitions

Controller: An employee, usually stationed in the control center, who is authorized and responsible for all rail operations. Duties may include, but are not limited to, train control, train dispatching, train supervision and related field activities.

Maintenance facility: The location within defined limits utilized by the RTS for the maintenance and repair of rail transit vehicles.

On-track equipment: A rail mounted vehicle or equipment, including high-rail vehicles and equipment, that is not used for revenue service but is used to inspect, maintain, and repair the rail system.

Line of sight: A mode of train operation in which the operator must visually ensure that it is safe to operate a train under various operating conditions and be able to stop the train prior to any obstruction.

Rail transit system (RTS): An organization that operates passenger train service and its supporting activities.

3.4 Emergency Management

3.4.1 Emergency Planning

LU's emergency planning and response process has been designed to ensure that LU manages incidents safely and restores service as soon as practical and as safely possible. LU has had to respond to a variety of internal and external incidents over the past five years. As a result, LU has amended and improved its processes, co-ordination internally and with third parties, training and emergency planning. The information below outlines some of these systems in more detail.

LU's requirements for emergency planning and related arrangements are contained in the Manager's Handbook (Providing emergency, contingency and business continuity and security support) covering:

- Emergency preparedness plans.
- Planning table-top exercises.
- Planning live emergency exercises.
- Planning emergency leap frog exercises.

LU ensures that its employees are trained and prepared through emergency planning arrangements through specific post and competency requirements, training modules and participation in emergency exercises.

The Manager's Handbook requires production of emergency plans that define individual roles and responsibilities in degraded and emergency conditions. It also establishes arrangements that provide fast and effective response to all types of incident. Suppliers are required to produce emergency plans through clauses in their contracts.

LU has three levels of emergency plan:
- The LU Network Plan which covers incidents that may affect a number of lines or the entire LU network involving stations and trains, e. g. major power failure, major loss of communications systems, major flooding and terrorist attack.
- Line plans which cover incidents (stations and trains) that may affect specific lines, and form part of each Service Delivery Unit's Emergency Plan, e. g. stalled trains or loss of local signalling or power control.
- Local plans which cover specific locations, e. g. stations, service control centres, train crew depots, e. g. station evacuation due to congestion or local security alert.

All emergency plans are integrated and mutually support one another. The findings of the risk assessment process are used to structure the content of these plans, as necessary. Rules dealing with operational emergencies and incidents are documented in the various rules books. Where required, third parties, such as TRANSEC (the Department of Transport's Transport Security Team), emergency services, large event organisers or other transport undertakings, are involved in the development of LU's emergency plans. This closer working, including joint development of congestion control and emergency plans at LU stations, has allowed LU to build more robust and effective emergency plans.

Whilst LU involves the emergency services in exercises in respect of these plans, emergency plans are not, by agreement, routinely provided as they are predominantly for the utilisation of LU staff and managers. However, stations' fire compliance plans are made available to the fire service. These plans and the axonometric diagrams show the physical layout and configuration of sub-surface stations including the fire precautions and controls. These plans are maintained by the access team in the network services team.

In the event of an on-train emergency, customers are evacuated by train staff assisted by station staff as appropriate. LU procedures assume that escape is only possible through the end cab doors and a "break glass" cover is provided over the cab door handle accessible from the passenger saloon to facilitate this. All resident station employees are trained to handle emergencies at their station and the stations in the area they cover.

Staff are trained to handle a comprehensive range of emergencies as required by the rule books as part of the continuous development training. Managers receive training for dealing with emergencies that are appropriate to their post. All operational employees also undertake fire training.

LU's mobile communication system (connect) allows communication across all aspects of the network during normal and degraded operations.

Live emergency leap-frog exercises are carried out at least once a year for each line with one-person operated trains in tube tunnel sections (except for those lines with full automatic train operation). Third parties are involved in these exercises where appropriate.

3.4.2 Incident Response and Recovery

Incidents on the LU network are managed in accordance with emergency planning arrangements (described above). LU has established an incident organisation structure (set out in the LU rule book) for incident organisation and management. This defines the roles of all those involved in incident response and sets out the arrangements that are put into place following an incident.

The aim of these arrangements is to safeguard customers and employees by establishing an organisation which will provide fast and effective responses to all types of incident, achieve the objective of incident containment, minimise injury/loss and restore LU operations as quickly as possible.

The rule book sets requirements for:
- Initial actions following an incident.
- Cooperation with others, including Tube Lines and its role.
- Roles, responsibilities and actions.
- Incident control structure, including a "gold, silver, bronze" control structure.
- Preservation of evidence.
- Additional arrangements in respect of particularly serious or protracted incidents.
- Special events requiring the implementation of incident control arrangements.
- Interfaces with Network Rail and other operating companies.

Effective communication is managed through clear identification of responsibilities as set out in the Formal Incident Management system set out in the Rule Book.

A senior LU manager is available on-call at all times to undertake the role of Rostered Duty Officer (RDO). The RDO assumes overall command during an incident and is responsible for formulating the strategy for dealing with the incident and its effects on other LU services outside of the incident site.

Following an incident that requires formal incident organisation, the RDO is contacted by the LU Network Operations Centre (NOC). The NOC acts as the link between the RDO and those directly managing/handling the incident. Where necessary, the NOC also call out the Emergency Response Unit (ERU) and advises the Office of Rail Regulation (ORR) (TfL Team), Rail Accident Investigation Branch (RAIB) and others as appropriate.

The LU Head of Engineering and Tube Lines also maintain rosters of on-call engineering support for incidents in the form of Duty Engineers.

The ERU, managed by Tube Lines, provides emergency response capability across the whole LU network. The provision of this service is managed through the contract with Tube Lines, and specifically the ERU agreement that forms part of the PPP Contract.

The equipment that the ERU is required to maintain is listed in the ERU Agreement.

The ERU is available to attend incidents on 24-hour standby basis and is trained to deal with all foreseeable rail related incidents across the LU network. Through mutual aid agreements, the ERU supports Network Rail when incidents occur on its infrastructure.

The ERU is also contractually obliged to partake in a minimum of one live emergency exercise per year.

For incidents involving other infrastructure managers and train operating companies (either on or adjacent to other infrastructure), TfL/LU employees work jointly with other relevant organisations to deal with the initial incident and investigation. If an incident occurs on network rail property, then the network rail emergency plan comes into operation.

Incident Recovery

For incidents that require significant or protracted recovery arrangements outside the scope of the incident organisation, LU has established an emergency recovery process within the LU network plan. Once such an incident has been dealt with via the arrangements for incident organisation described above, the emergency recovery process is initiated via the relevant line general manager working with the emergency planning manager. In the event that the impact of the incident has implications beyond the line, the duty director is notified in order to initiate the recovery process at network level.

Where it is established that an emergency recovery response team is required, this is established by the relevant senior manager in conjunction with the Emergency Planning Manager. The extent of the arrangements and composition of the team reflects the nature and scale of the incident. Those involved act as the link between the team and their area of LU that is providing recovery support. The role of the team is to assess what is required in order to return LU lines or network services to normal operation, and developing the arrangements to achieve this including priorities, strategy, funding requirements and additional resourcing needs.

The requirements for undertaking a post-incident assessment and developing and delivering the recovery plan are embodied in the LU Network Plan.

Definitions

Safety stops: Stops made to verify the braking capability of a train to enhance safety in advance of an RTS defined must-stop situation.

Storage Incident: An undesired event that results in, or under slightly different circumstances could have resulted in, harm to people, damage to property, damage to the environment, or loss of process.

Infrastructure manager: Has the meaning ascribed to it by the Railways and Other Guided Transport Systems (Safety) Regulations.

Interlocking machine rooms: A large signalling equipment room which houses the equipment associated with the signalling interlocking system.

LU group: LU, Tube Lines, PFI suppliers and other suppliers.

LU network: The geographic extent of the services provided by London Underground.

LUCAS: London Underground Combined Access System (LUCAS) is the membership and smartcard scheme for engineering and construction workers on London Underground.

Station control room: Room on a station from which the station is controlled on a minute by minute basis.

Railway group: Organisations that are bound to comply with Railway Group Standards.

Station control room: Room on a station from which the station is controlled on a minute by minute basis.

Railway group: Organisations that are bound to comply with Railway Group Standards.

Railway group standards: Standards mandated by Railway Safety and Standards Board (RSSB) for use by organisations that operate on or support the operations of Network Rails' infrastructure.

Responsibility: Normally assigned to the person who undertakes the activity, the "doer". The person may delegate the task or a part thereof to another or contract the work to a third party, but retains responsibility for the outcome.

Risk profile: A graphical representation of LU's "Top Events".

Tracks: Those tracks upon where trains are stored.

Train: A rail mounted vehicle that is used or intended to be used in revenue service — any motorcar, locomotive or other self-propelled on-rail vehicle, with or without other cars coupled.

Train operator: An authorized onboard employee who controls the movement of a train.

Yard: A facility within defined limits that has a system of tracks used for making up trains, storing trains and other purposes. A maintenance facility may be included.

Yard supervisor: One who oversees the activity of work or workers in the yard.

Yard tracks: All tracks, other than mainline tracks, contained within the limits of the yard.

3.4.3 Fatal Accident

At about 10:10 on 26 May 2020, at Waterloo Underground station in London, a passenger fell into the gap between the northbound Bakerloo line platform and the train from which he had just alighted. A large gap existed between the train and the platform because of the track curvature at the location of the passenger's fall. The passenger was unable to free himself and the train departed with the passenger still in the gap, crushing him as it moved off. He remained motionless on the track and was subsequently hit by a second train that entered the station.

The accident occurred when there were no staff or other members of public nearby to assist the fallen passenger. Train despatch on the Bakerloo line platforms at Waterloo was undertaken by the train operator (driver) using a closed-circuit television system to view the side of the train alongside the platform. With only his head and arm above platform level, the passenger was difficult to detect on the despatch monitors, and was not seen by the train operator. The operator of the following train was unaware of the passenger because their attention was focused on the platform and the train's stopping point, until after the train had struck the passenger.

The investigation found that London Underground's risk assessment processes did not enable the identification and detailed assessment of all factors that contributed to higher platform-train interface (PTI) risk at certain platforms. Consequently, although London Underground had implemented some location-specific mitigation measures at the PTI, it had not fully quantified the contribution of curved platforms to the overall PTI risk, and so was unable to fully assess the potential benefits of additional mitigation at these locations.

The investigation also found that the model used by London Underground to quantify system risk makes no allowance for non-fatal injuries, and so understates the risk of harm to passengers at the PTI and presents an incomplete picture of system risk, with the potential to affect London Underground's safety decision making. RAIB has made three recommendations to London Underground. The first relates to the need to recognise and assess location-specific risks so they can be properly managed.

The second deals with the need to ensure that safety management processes include the ongoing evaluation of existing safety measures at stations, and provide periodic risk assessment for individual locations at intervals which reflect the level of risk present. The third recommendation relates to the need for effective delivery of actions proposed by internal investigation recommendations.

Trains and Equipment Involved

The accident involved two northbound Bakerloo line trains which had begun their journeys at Elephant and Castle station. The first, train running number 210, started its journey at about 10:00 and the second, train running number 214, three minutes later.

Both trains were formed of 1972 tube stock and consisted of 3-carriage and 4-carriage units operating as 7-carriage trains. Each carriage is about 16 meters long with two double doorways approximately one-third and two-thirds of the way along the carriage length, and single doorways at each end, as shown in figure 3.17. The fourth carriage of the incident train incorporated a driving cab, so did not have a single doorway at the leading end.

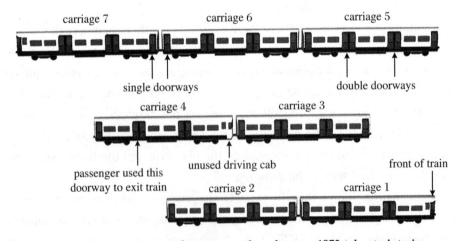

Figure 3.17　Arrangement of passenger saloon doors on 1972 tube stock trains

Bakerloo line trains are driven manually by a train operator. Train operators undertake platform despatch duties with assistance from either a CCTV system using cameras with platform-mounted monitors positioned in the operator's eyeline, or platform-mounted mirrors targeted on the platform-train interface (PTI). LUL does not require station platforms on its network to be staffed at all times, but defines times when this is needed at some stations. However, LUL had arrangements in place to provide staff on certain platforms at busy times to assist passengers and expedite the flow of people, and the movement of trains in and out of the station. In such circumstances, operators are taught to stop their train if an emergency signal is given by staff on the station platform.

Platform 3 at Waterloo was equipped with a CCTV system because the track curvature limited the view along the train, as shown in figure 3.18. This CCTV system was independent of the station CCTV system and comprised six cameras, each feeding a single monitor. The overlapping images on the monitors allowed train operators to view the PTI along the full length of their train. These monitors, known as One Person Operation (OPO) monitors, were located just inside the tunnel mouth at the departure end of the platform. In the event of a failure of the OPO system, platform staff must be provided to assist the train operator with the safe despatch of trains.

Figure 3.18 OPO monitors provided inside the tunnel at Waterloo Bakerloo line platform 3

3.5 Writing: How to Write Job Applications

Employers may receive hundreds of applications for a job, so it's vital to make sure that the letter or email you send with your resume creates the right impression. It's your opportunity to say why you want the job, and to present yourself as a candidate for the post in a way that impresses a prospective employer and makes you stand out as a prospective employee.

Before you start: read the advert closely so that you can tailor your application to the requirements of the job. Research the organization: this will show prospective employers that you really are interested in them. Composing the letter or email.

General points:
- Keep it brief. You don't need to give a lot of detail. What you are aiming for is a clear and concise explanation of your suitability for the job.
- Begin your letter or email "Dear Mr/Mrs/Ms xxxx" if you know the person's name, or "Dear Sir or Madam" if you don't know their name.
- Avoid inappropriate language such as slang or technical jargon.
- Use brief, informative sentences and short paragraphs.
- Check your spelling, grammar, and punctuation carefully. Some employers routinely discard job applications that contain such mistakes.

The usual structures of a job application letter or email are as follows.

The position applied for: give the title of the job as a heading, or refer to it in the first sentence of your letter, using the reference code if there is one. This will ensure that your application goes directly to the right person in the organization. You should also mention where you saw the job advert or where you heard about the vacancy. If you heard about it through someone already working for the company, mention their name and position.

Your current situation: if you're working, briefly outline your current job. Pick up on the job requirements outlined in the advert and focus on any of your current skills or responsibilities that correspond to those requested. For example, if the advert states that management skills are essential, then state briefly what management experience you have. If you're still studying, focus on the relevant aspects or modules of your course.

Your reasons for wanting the job: be clear and positive about why you want the job. You might feel that you are ready for greater challenges, more responsibility, or a change of direction, for example. Outline the qualities and skills that you believe you can bring to the job or organization.

Closing paragraph: in the final paragraph you could say when you'd be available to start work, or suggest that the company keep your resume on file if they decide you're not suitable for the current job.

Signature: if you are sending a letter rather than an email, always remember to sign it and to type your name underneath your signature.

Sample: Database Administrator.

Please write a letter to apply for the position of database administrator in H Company.

Dear Hiring Manager,

I am delighted for the opportunity to apply for the position of Database Administrator in H Company. I have enjoyed my time working as a database professional during my career, and I have met and solved many informational and data-related challenges in the process. I am always interested in acquiring better ways to improve database efficiency and performance, and I look forward to learning more about the goals that H Company wants to achieve in the feild of safe and secure data management.

As a Senior Database Administrator, I have maintained multiple database systems for my employers. While at former company I headed the team of database professionals whose jobs were to monitor, design and streamline all the repositories of data. This data was highly important and contained many personal details about our customers' financial information. I ensured that all safety protocols were followed and that best practices were implemented at all times.

Thank you for your consideration of my application. I am interested in hearing more details about the Database Administrator position and learning more about H Company. I am always ready to share my knowledge with others, and I love learning new things from my peers, especially in a fast-paced environment such as H Company.

I look forward to hearing from you in the near future.
Sincerely,
David

3.6 KEY TERMS

(1) terminal station

(2) intermediate station

(3) junction station

(4) connecting station

(5) island platform

(6) separate platform

(7) train operator

(8) the train's stopping point

(9) London Underground Limited (LUL)

(10) carriage units

(11) carriage trains

(12) emergency signal

(13) platform screen doors (PSD)
(14) platform edge doors (PEDs)
(15) half-height platform screen doors
(16) full-height platform screen doors
(17) sliding doors
(18) access door to tracks
(19) emergency egress door
(20) automatic train operation
(21) automatic gate
(22) contactless card/token
(23) ticket vending machine
(24) free area/unpaid area
(25) paid area
(26) station personnel
(27) platform telephones
(28) telecommunications device for the deaf (TDD)
(29) operations control center (OCC)
(30) station opening checklist
(31) station closing checklist
(32) turnback track
(33) loop track
(34) two-track terminus
(35) peak hours
(36) headway
(37) passengers per hour per direction (PPHPD)
(38) round trip time
(39) depot
(40) dwell times
(41) recovery time
(42) audible signals
(43) hand signals
(44) shunting operations
(45) train controllers
(46) on-track equipment (OTE)
(47) main tracks
(48) running tracks
(49) side tracks
(50) maintenance workers

(51) yard
(52) safety stops
(53) coupling cars
(54) uncoupling cars
(55) yard supervisors
(56) on-track equipment (OTE)
(57) rail transit system (RTS)
(58) emergency preparedness plans
(59) stalled trains
(60) local signalling
(61) contactless
(62) sub-surface stations
(63) on-train emergency
(64) one-person operated trains (OPO)
(65) train-kilometre
(66) train operations manager (TOM)

3.7 EXERCISES

I Match the terms with correct definitions or explanations.

| dwell time   recovery time   operations control center   loop
| station control room   controller yard   terminal station   headway
| siding/side track |

1. Time built into a schedule between arrivals and departures, used for the recovery of delays and preparation for the return trip. (   )

2. In transportation planning, the time duration of a linked trip, that is, from the point of origin to the final destination, including waiting and walking time at transfer points and trip ends. (   )

3. Room on a station from which the station is controlled on a minute by minute basis. (   )

4. The facility where rail operations such as train control, train dispatching, train supervision and related field activities are accomplished for the entire rail transit system or

for specific segments of a system if there is more than one such facility. (　)

5. A facility within defined limits that has a system of tracks used for making up trains, storing trains and other purposes. A maintenance facility may be included. (　)

6. An employee, usually stationed in the control center, who is authorized and responsible for all rail operations. Duties may include, but are not limited to, train control, train dispatching, train supervision and related field activities. (　)

7. This generally refers to stations at the end of lines, but includes stations in the middle of networks where most trains terminate their journeys. (　)

8. A track adjacent to a main or a secondary track, for meeting, passing, or storing cars or trains. (　)

9. In rail operations, a point along a track at which a train may reverse direction.
(　)

10. A transit route or guideway layout that is of a closed continuous form, such as a circle. A terminal track layout or bus driveway that reverses the direction of a vehicle without the vehicle's reversing. (　)

11. The time interval between the passing of the front ends of successive transit units (vehicles or trains) moving along the same lane or track (or other guideway) in the same direction, usually expressed in minutes; see also service frequency. (　)

Ⅱ　Answer the following questions according to the text.
1. Compare the differences between island platform and separate platform.

2. Describe the architecture of the AFC system.

3. Explain the round trip time.

4. Describe the requirements of safe operations in the yard and maintenance facility.

Chapter 4 Subway Train

> A modern passenger multiple unit train is usually made up of a number of inter-dependent vehicles which cannot operate unless all the vehicles are of the right type and are coupled in the correct position in the train. Power and auxiliary equipment is usually distributed under more than one vehicle and is all controlled from the driving position. Vehicles in multiple units are usually referred to as "cars" and are known as "motor cars" if powered and "trailer cars" if not.
>
> A six-car train comprises two three-car units. These units are coupled by a semi permanent bar coupler, but can be driven as a three-car train for non-operational purposes. Figure 4.1 shows typical types of electric multiple units, example 1 shows a 3-car unit with 66% axles motored, example 2 shows a 4-car unit with 25% axles motored, example 3 has a 4-car unit with 37.5% axles motored.

In China, generally, three-car unit comprises:
- A trailer car, equipped with a cabin (DT or TC).
- A motor vehicle, equipped with a pantograph (DM or Mp).
- A motor vehicle-intermediate (M).

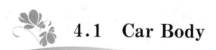
4.1 Car Body

The bodyshell is a welded aluminum fabrication with a stainless steel fire barrier in the floor.

The passenger areas are laid out to achieve maximum standing areas while providing 50 seats arranged along the sidewall. Two rows of ceiling mounted fluorescent lights extend the length of the saloons, with emergency lights positioned above the doors and gangways. Both the normal and emergency lighting are powered by two independent circuits. This split circuit reduces the risk of total lighting failure.

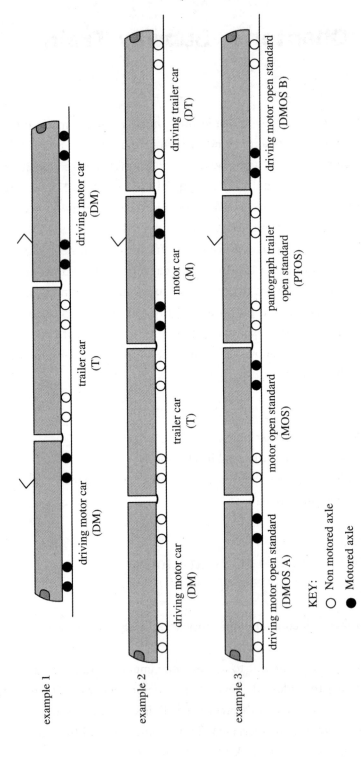

Figure 4.1 Schematics showing typical types of electric multiple units (EMUs)

Passenger comfort is maintained by ventilation and air-conditioning system and a comprehensive communications system provides audio information.

Access to the train for disabled passengers is facilitated by level boarding between the platform and the train floor. Two seats have been removed in each Mp car to provide a secure location for wheelchair bound passengers.

4.2 Bogie

Bogies come in many shapes and sizes but it is in its most developed form as the motor bogie of an electric or diesel locomotive or an EMU. Generally, there are two categories of bogies: the motor bogie and the trailer bogie.

4.2.1 The Motor Bogie

The motor bogie carries two traction motors and two gearboxes, each driving one axle. The traction motors are bolted to the axle frame and are connected to the gearboxes that are mounted on the axle, via a flexible coupling.

A passenger bogie also has springs mounted on the top of the axle boxes of the wheelsets. These axlebox springs are known as the primary suspension. The air springs are known as the secondary suspension. The car body is therefore separated from the track by two sets of springs (figure 4.2).

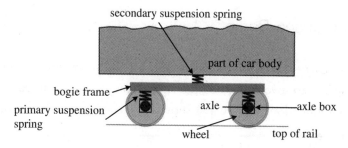

Figure 4.2 Simple schematic of passenger car suspension system showing the general arrangement and location of the primary suspension springs on the axle boxes and the secondary suspension upon which the car body rests

In some cases, the axle box is mounted on a swing arm that is attached to the bogie frame, the free end of the swing arm mounts the primary suspension — a coil spring and a hydraulic damper.

Secondary suspension air bag, mounted on the steel frame of the bogie, with hydraulic vertical dampers in parallel, provide secondary suspension. They allow for rotation of the bogie about the traction centre and maintain the height of the car (figure 4.3).

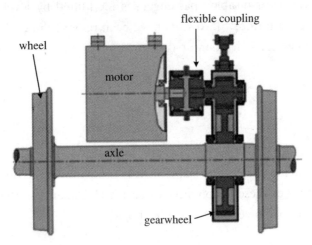

Figure 4.3 The traction equipment of bogie

The traction centre transmits traction and braking forces from the bogie to the car body via the centre pivot.

4.2.2 The Trailer Bogie

The trailer bogie is fitted to the Dt cars. They have no traction equipment, but Wheel Flange Lubrication fitted in order to reduce the wear on the wheel flange and noise at locations with small radius bends.

4.2.3 A high-speed Bogie

Here it has to carry the motors, brakes and suspension systems all within a tight envelope. It is subjected to severe stresses and shocks and may have to run at over 300 km/h in a high speed application. Figure 4.4 shows an electric traction motor bogie.

(1) Bogie Frame

It can be of steel plate or cast steel. In this case, it is a modern design of welded steel box format where the structure is formed into hollow sections of the required shape.

(2) Bogie Transom

Transverse structural member of bogie frame (usually two off) which also supports the carbody guidance parts and the traction motors.

(3) Brake Cylinder

An air brake cylinder is provided for each wheel. A cylinder can operate tread or disc brakes. Some designs incorporate parking brakes as well. Some bogies have two brake cylinders per wheel for heavy duty braking requirements. Each wheel is provided with a brake discon each side and a brake pad actuated by the brake cylinder. A pair of pads is hung from the bogie frame and activated by links attached to the piston in the brake cylinder. When air is admitted into the brake cylinder, the internal piston moves these links and causes the brake pads to press against the discs. A brake hanger support bracket carries the brake hangers, from which the pads are hung.

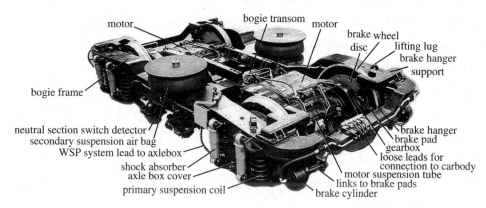

Figure 4.4 An electric traction motor bogie with a welded steel frame and nose suspended traction motors (A high speed bogie)

(4) Primary Suspension Coil

A steel coil spring, two of which are fitted to each axlebox in this design. They carry the weight of the bogie frame and anything attached to it.

(5) Motor Suspension Tube

Many motors are suspended between the transverse member of the bogie frame called the transom and the axle. This motor is called "nose suspended" because it is hung between the suspension tube and a single mounting on the bogie transom called the nose.

(6) Gearbox

This contains the pinion and gearwheel which connects the drive from the armature to the axle.

(7) Lifting Lug

Allows the bogie to be lifted by a crane without the need to tie chains or ropes around the frame.

(8) Motor

Normally, each axle has its own motor. It drives the axle through the gearbox. Some designs, particularly on tramcars, use a motor to drive two axles.

(9) Neutral Section Switch Detector

In the UK, the overhead line is divided into sections with short neutral sections separating them. It is necessary to switch off the current on the train while the neutral section is crossed. A magnetic device mounted on the track marks the start and finish of the neutral section. The device is detected by a box mounted on the leading bogie of the train to inform the equipment when to switch off and on.

(10) Secondary Suspension Air Bag

Rubber air suspension bags are provided as the secondary suspension system for most modern trains. The air is supplied from the train's compressed air system.

(11) Wheel Slide Protection System Lead to Axlebox

Where a Wheel Slide Protection (WSP) system is fitted, axle boxes are fitted with speed sensors. These are connected by means of a cable attached to the WSP box cover on the axle end.

(12) Loose Leads for Connection to Carbody

The motor circuits are connected to the traction equipment in the car or locomotive by flexible leads shown here.

(13) Shock Absorber

To reduce the effects of vibration occurring as a result of the wheel/rail interface.

(14) Axlebox Cover

Simple protection for the return current brush, if fitted, and the axle bearing lubrication.

4.3 Brake System

There are two braking systems on the train: electric regenerative brake and pneumatic brake. Figure 4.5 shows the principal parts of the air brake system.

4.3.1 Electric Regenerative Brake

The principal braking method is regenerative braking. Under normal operation in automatic operating mode, brake effort is provided by operating the traction motors in reverse. This generates alternating current that is converted to direct current and fed back into the overhead line. This braking effort is supplemented by the application of the friction brake up to the level required by the ATO system.

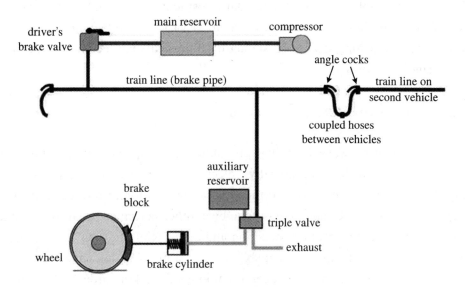

Figure 4.5 The air brake system

4.3.2 Pneumatic Brake

Pneumatic friction braking is achieved by forcing brake blocks against the wheel treads. Friction braking is used:

In emergency braking.

When the overhead line is not 10 receptive to power.

To blend with the electric brake during service braking to maintain smooth braking.

To provide all brake effort at low speeds when regenerative braking does not occur.

In the event of failure of the electric brake, the friction brake is fully rated for the brake operational duty. The air supply for the friction brakes is provided from the MR pipe via the brake reservoirs, located on the underframe at the ends of each car.

4.4 Couplers

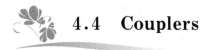

4.4.1 Introduction

In order for two railway vehicles to be connected together in a train they are provided with couplers. Since there are a large number of railway vehicles which might have to be coupled at one time or another in their lives, it would seem sensible to ensure that the couplers are compatible and are at a standard position on each end of each vehicle. Of course, life isn't as simple as that, so there are a variety of different couplers around. However, there is a high degree of standardisation and some common types have appeared around the world.

4.4.2 Fully Automatic Couplers

More and more railways are using fully automatic couplers. A fully automatic coupler connects the vehicles mechanically, electrically and pneumatically, normally by pushing the two vehicles together and then operating a button or foot pedal in the cab to complete the operation. Uncoupling is done by another button or pedal to disconnect the electrical contact and pneumatic connection and disengaging the coupler mechanically.

Fully automatic couplers are complex and need a lot of maintenance care and attention. They need to be used often to keep them in good working order. There are a number of different designs in use.

The Scharfenberg automatic coupler figure 4.6 is a design widely used on European multiple unit rolling stock of all types, ranging from high speed trains to light rail vehicles. The coupler has a mechanical portion with pneumatic and electrical connections. The units are coupled by pushing one onto the other. The electrical contacts mounted under the mechanical coupler are protected by a cover when uncoupled.

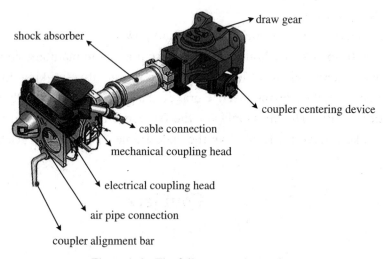

Figure 4.6 The fully automatic coupler

4.5 Traction System

4.5.1 Power Supply and Propulsion System

The power supply is collected from the 1500 V DC overhead line by a single arm pantograph, mounted on the roof of each of the Mp cars. Each pantograph supplies power to the two propulsion inverters mounted on each Mp car of the half set. In turn, each propulsion inverter feeds two 3-phase AC induction traction motors on one bogie.

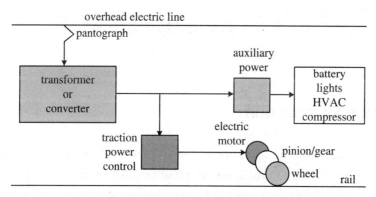

Figure 4.7　The traction system

4.5.2 The Auxiliary Power System

The 1500 V DC input is applied to the auxiliary converter on the Mp car. The output from the auxiliary converter is passed to the Auxiliary Transformer on the Mi car. This transformer provides the following:

Electrical isolation between the 1500 V DC traction supply and the 400 V AC auxiliary supply. This arrangement ensures that under fault conditions, the 1500 V supply cannot be connected to the auxiliary bus line.

A star connected secondary, producing a 400 V 3-phase supply for battery charging and auxiliary supplies together with a 230 V single phase supply. The 400 V 3-phase supply is required for: air conditioning, fan motor, compressor motor, and battery charger.

4.5.3 DC Loads

The 3-phase AC supply from the Auxiliary Transformer is rectified by a six diode bridge to produce a relatively smooth DC current. It is then filtered to remove transients before being converted to single phase AC by the inverter. This is then transformed to 110 V before being rectified and filtered to produce the DC voltage required for the train loads and battery charging. Train batteries and battery chargers are located on the underframes of all cars.

The following loads are supplied by the train batteries: head/tail lights, automate train control, coupler control, wake up control, and auxiliary compressor.

4.6 Train Operation

4.6.1 Basic Introduction

This section describes the train operation of Victoria Line of London Underground. The train was formed of 2009 tube stock that had recently been introduced into service on the Victoria Line as part of an upgrade of the trains and signalling. Each train consists of eight cars, made up from two four-car units that are semi-permanently coupled together and can accommodate 252 seated passengers and 1196 standing passengers. The total length of a train is 133.28 metres.

On each car there is a set of double sliding doors at a third and two thirds of the way along each side. In addition, the cars without a driving cab have single leaf sliding doors giving access to the passenger saloon at each end; cars with a driving cab have single leaf sliding doors giving access to the saloon at the non-cab end.

The trains normally operate in automatic mode and only require the train operator to open the doors on arrival at a station, and then close the doors and press the start buttons (figure 4.8) if it is safe for the train to depart.

4.6.2 Train Door Systems

The train doors are hung on the outside of the cars (figure 4.9), and are driven open and closed by electric motors that are controlled by electronic door control units. The doors incorporate an obstacle detection system to detect large objects that prevent the doors fully closing, and a sensitive edge system to detect thin objects that have been trapped by the fully. The obstacle detection system works when the train operator closes the doors. Should a closing door encounter an obstruction, it will stop and reopen by 25 mm to 75 mm, then pause for 0.5 seconds before attempting to reclose again. If the obstruction remains, the door will make two further attempts to close by opening and then closing again, and the train will be prevented from obtaining traction power.

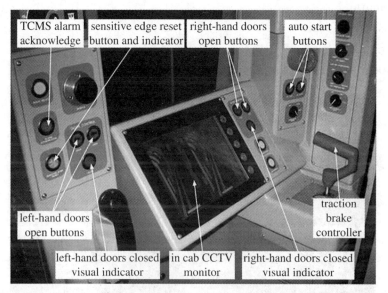

Figure 4.8　Layout of relevant cab controls in the driving cab of 2009 tube stock

Figure 4.9　Northbound platform at Warren Street, Victoria Line

The train operator can only get traction power to start the train if an electrical circuit, known as the train doors interlock circuit, is completed. This is achieved when all the train doors are fully closed and proved to be closed. This is indicated to the train operator by the illumination of the doors closed visual indicator.

4.6.3 Driving Modes

The 2009 tube stock can be driven in the following modes:
① Automatic.
② Protected manual.
③ Restricted manual.
Each mode is selected using the master control switch (figure 4.10).

Figure 4.10 Master control switch 2009 tube stock

The normal mode in passenger service is "automatic" in which the system accelerates, brakes and accurately stops the train, as required, after the train operator has pressed the two start buttons. This is known as automatic train operation (ATO). The train is prevented from colliding with another train by a system called automatic train protection (ATP).

The manual modes of driving are the "protected" and "restricted" modes and are used following the occurrence of some fault conditions and while driving within the limits of the depot at Northumberland Park. The manual modes are not normally used while trains are in passenger service. In the protected mode, the train is prevented from colliding with other trains by the ATP system and the maximum permitted speed is 80 km/h. ATP is not available in the restricted mode where the maximum permitted speed is limited to 16 km/h. In order to use the manual driving modes, the train operator must operate the master control switch to the appropriate position and then drive the train using the traction brake controller (figure 4.10).

4.6.4 Train Control Management System (TCMS)

The TCMS is an on-train computer system which monitors, records and displays fault and other event conditions associated with a train's electrical and electronic control systems. The interface between the TCMS and the train operator is a touch sensitive display screen in the driving cab, which allows the train operator to view data displayed by the TCMS and to respond appropriately to the information provided.

The TCMS provides messages about the condition of the train and suggests technical actions that the train operator should take in response. It does not include operational procedures, because these are likely to change periodically and are covered by training and briefing.

There are three categories of messaging based on the impact of the event on the train and the ability of the train operator to take any action in response. The event category, decided by a group made up of LUL and Bombardier representatives, determines whether the message will be displayed immediately or when the train is next stationary at a station. The messages are accompanied by an audible alarm which the train operator must acknowledge. There is a further category of message known as an operational advisory which is accompanied by an audible single momentary alert. For events causing an alarm, which the train operator has acknowledged, the message displayed on the TCMS screen can be cleared from the screen by acknowledging the touch screen button, once the cause of the message has been resolved.

4.7 KEY TERMS

(1) coupler
(2) trailer
(3) pantograph
(4) ventilation
(5) electric multiple unit (EMU)
(6) stainless steel
(7) a six-car train
(8) bogie
(9) trailer bogie

(10) motor bogie
(11) axle
(12) bolt
(13) coupling
(14) wheel flange
(15) lubrication
(16) wear
(17) wear and tear
(18) small radius bend
(19) primary suspension
(20) coil spring
(21) damper
(22) braking force
(23) regenerative brake
(24) pneumatic brake
(25) alternating current
(26) service braking
(27) direct current
(28) brake block
(29) wheel tread
(30) emergency braking
(31) main reservoir pipe (MR pipe)
(32) brake reservoir
(33) traction
(34) overhead line
(35) propulsion inverter
(36) 3-phase AC induction traction motors
(37) auxiliary inverter
(38) converter
(39) transformer
(40) fault condition
(41) bus line
(42) air conditioning
(43) compressor
(44) rectify
(45) diode
(46) six diode bridge
(47) voltage

(48) underframe
(49) head light
(50) tail light
(51) wake up control
(52) train control management system (TCMS)
(53) driving modes

4.8 EXERCISES

I Match the terms with correct definitions or explanations.

| bogie   regenerative brake   coupler   service braking |

1. In rail transportation, a rail vehicle component that consists of a frame, normally two axles, brakes, suspension, and other parts, which supports the vehicle body and can swivel under it on curves.   (   )

2. A form of dynamic brake in which the electrical energy generated by braking is returned to the power supply line instead of being dissipated in resistors.   (   )

3. A device for connecting one rail vehicle to another. The mechanism is usually placed in a standard location at both ends of all rail cars and locomotives.   (   )

4. A non-emergency brake application the obtains the maximum brake rate that is consistent with the design of the brake system, retrievable under the control of master control.   (   )

II Answer the following questions according to the text.

1. Please describe the main difference of the trailer bogie and motor bogie.

2. Please describe the principle of regenerative braking.

3. Please describe the principle of power supply and propulsion system of subway train.

4. Please list the main driving mode of subway trains.

Chapter 5 Electromechanical Equipment

> Electromechanical equipment is an important part of urban rail transit system and plays an important role. Electromechanical equipment for the subway station can transport passengers quickly, ensure the safety of passengers, improve environment of the station, assist the station to operate and manage. The quality of electromechanical equipment directly determines the service quality of the station.

5.1 Platform Screen Door

5.1.1 Overview of the PSD

Platform screen door (abbreviated as PSD) is an advanced electromechanical equipment for rail transit station which is developed in the 1980s. The Lille Metro was first one to install PSD in the world. The heavy railway system of the Singapore Metro, which opened in 1987, also used PSD and the railway systems in Europe and Asia have been introduced to install PSD, so that system of PSD becomes one of the standards of the current subway system, as shown in figure 5.1.

Chinese first subway line to install PSD is Guangzhou Metro Line 2, whereafter subway lines in other cities, such as Shanghai, Shenzhen, Tianjin, Beijing and so on, began to introduce PSD. Because of research and development of PSD, many companies gradually have core technology of PSD, which marks foreign technology monopoly had been broken. Shenzhen metro line 1 is the first one to install the PSD developed by Shenzhen Fangda Group. Now Shenzhen Fangda Group is the leader in the production of PSD.

As many technologies, such as the combination of computer network technology and embedded system, are continually innovating in PSD, the PSD comes to be the essential equipment which must be installed in subway station. The PSD can create a safer and more comfortable environment for passengers. What is PSD? It setting at the edge of the platform, separates the subway station into passenger area and railway area and synchronize sliding door with train gate by opening and closing the sliding door continuously. Therefore, the PSD is a comprehensive electromechanical equipment which integrates many kinds of technologies, such as architecture, mechanics, electronic engineering, automation control technology, computer network technology and other disciplines. It is permanently located in the urban rail transit, rail transit, light rail and other rail transit stations.

Figure 5.1　London Underground, UK

5.1.2　Type of PSD

(1) Airtight PSD

The airtight PSD is a fully enclosed glass partition or gate installed from the top of the station to the edge of the station platform, completely separating the waiting area, as shown in figure 5.2. The subway station is surrounded with glass door of airtight PSD

Figure 5.2　Airtight PSD

which separates passenger area from subway station. It can not only prevent the crowd falling into the train area but also reduce the energy consumption of subway station. So the modern station features safe, energy-saving and comfortable. The airtight PSD completely separates the waiting area of the station from the train operation area, which not only avoids the crowding or accident of passengers from falling into the track, but also reduces the energy consumption of subway station, and provides passengers with a safe, energy-saving and comfortable environment for riding.

The earliest subway line using the airtight PSD in China is Guangzhou Metro Line 2. According to the statistics of Guangzhou Metro, the energy consumption of air conditioning in the station is saved by more than 20% after installing the airtight PSD.

(2) Non-airtight PSD

Non-airtight PSD is that does not completely isolate the passenger area from airspace of station. Non-airtight PSD has two types: whole-high PSD and semi-high PSD.

Whole-high PSD, compared with the airtight PSD, has same structural type. There is a gap between the top of PSD and bottom of beam. The gap can ventilate the subway station and reduce the pressure on door body, as shown in figure 5.3. The whole-high PSD has put into operation in many cities, such as Beijing metro, Nanjing metro, Xi'an metro and so on. The door body of the whole-high PSD is generally 2.4~2.6 m high, with 0.5 m gap between the top of PSD and bottom of beam. Because the passenger area and the train area are not completely separated, there is air flow between the platform and the station, the whole-high platform screen cannot has absolute function of energy saving and noise reduction. However, it still can avoid passengers to fall into the track.

Figure 5.3　The whole-high PSD

The door body structure of the semi-high PSD is generally 1.2~1.7 m and installed on the edge of the platform to separate the platform area from the track area. The main purpose is to improve securities. Compared with the the whole-high PSD, its main functions and features are to prevent passengers from crowding into and accidentally falling off the platform. At the same time, the semi-high PSD also has the advantages of simple and fast installation, less engineering interface, low cost, and short construction cycle. As shown in figure 5.4.

Figure 5.4 Semi-high-type PSD

The semi-high PSD is generally used for ground stations or elevated stations. Such as in Hefei Metro Line 3, Guangzhou Metro Line 4, Shanghai Metro Line 1 and so on.

5.1.3 Component and Function of PSD

PSD is a kind of mechanical and electrical equipment used in urban rail transit stations, mainly divided into mechanical and electrical parts. Mechanical part mainly includes door body structure (as shown in figure 5.5) and door machine system (as shown in figure 5.6); electrical part mainly includes control system, power supply system and monitoring system.

The functions of PSD is mainly to ensure safety, reduce energy consumption, improve the waiting environment, reduce operation costs, and improve the image of the city.

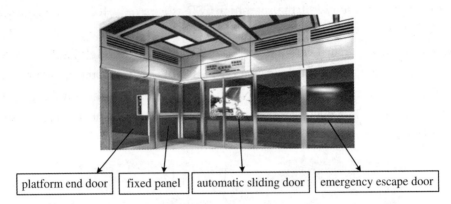

Figure 5.5　Component of PSD

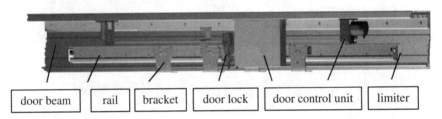

Figure 5.6　Door machine system

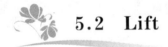

5.2.1　Overview of Lift

Long before, some original lifts were used to transport people and goods. Around 1100 BC, the ancient Chinese people invented the pulley, which used the rotary motion to complete the lifting motion for raising the goods. As shown in figure 5.7. In 236 BC, the Greek mathematician Archimedes designed and produced a lifting device consisting of winches and pulley sets. The driving force of these lifting tools is generally human or animal power. In the beginning of the 19th century, the lifting tool start to use the steam in Europe and America. In 1845, William Thomson developed a lift which is driven by water. Although the lifts were constantly improved by generations of innovative engineers, the lifts widely recognized by industry did not appear until the world's first safety lift was born in 1852. In 1889, the lifts had electric drive system and electric lift appeared, as shown in figure 5.8.

Figure 5.7 Pulley 　　　　　　　　　Figure 5.8 Lifting tool

Though the development of drive control technology, the lift went through many stages or phases. (DC motor driving, AC single speed control, two speed AC electric driving, DC gearless driving, AC driving, AC frequency conversion control). At the end of the 19th century, the DC lifts with the Ward-Leonard system appeared, which significantly improved the working efficiency of the lift. In the early part of the 20th century, the lift driven by AC induction motor was born. In the first half of the 20th century, a large of proportion of middle-speed lift and high-speed lift use DC speed regulation system to govern speed. In 1967, thyristor was born and applied to control system of lift, then the lift driven by using AC voltage regulation appeared. In 1983, the lift with AC frequency conversion control system quickly became a mainstream product in the market, the lift features steady running, strong security, energy conservation. The system is able to make passengers more reliable and more comfortable for customers. In 1996, the lift driven by the gearless traction machine is born and constantly develops. As the tractor and control cabinet are placed on the surface of the shaft, the independent machine room is unnecessary for operation of lift. This type of lift can save building costs and increase utilization rate of shaft. It also possesses the advantages of high efficiency, energy saving, no pollution, high stability and security. The modern lift has many types of control system, such as manual operation, push-buttons control, collective selective control, parallel control and group control and so on. Now lift company has been continuously researching and developing new features in order to meet the evolving needs of users. As shown in figure 5.9.

Figure 5.9 Modern lift

5.2.2 Component and Function of Lift

The lift consists of traction system, guidance system, car, door system, weight balance system, electric drive system, electrical control system, and safety protection system. As shown in table 5.1 and figure 5.10.

Table 5.1 Component of lift

Structure name	structural function	structural composition
Traction system	To output and transmit power to make the lift operate	Traction machine, traction wire rope, guide wheel and reverse rope wheel
Guidance system	To limit the car and the freedom of movement of the weight, so that the car and the weight can only lift the movement along the guide rail	Guide rails, guide boots and guide rails
Car	The lift assembly for transporting passengers and goods and the working part of the lift	A car frame and a car body
Door system	To seal the floor station entrance and the car entrance	Car door, floor door, door opening machine and door lock device
Weight balance system	To balance the weight of the car relatively and kept within the limit to ensure the normal traction drive of the lift	Counterweight and weight compensation devices

Continued

Structure name	structural function	structural composition
Electric drive system	To provide power and implement the lift speed control	Traction motor, power supply system, speed feedback device
Electrical control system	To operate and control the operation of the lift	Control device, position display device, control screen (cabinet), flat layer device, layer picker, etc.
Safety protection system	To ensure the safe use of the lift, to prevent all accidents endangering personal safety	Lift speed limiter, safety clamp, rope clamp, buffer, safety touch pad, layer door lock, lift safety window, lift overload limit device, limit switch device

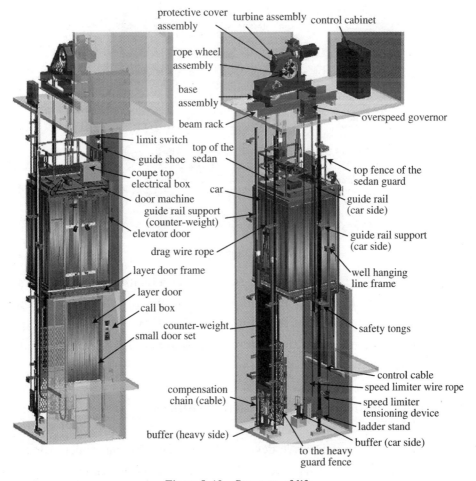

Figure 5.10 Structure of lift

5.3 Escalator

5.3.1 Overview of Escalator

In 1859, American Nason. Amuse invented a "rotary escalator" (As shown in figure 5.11). The rotary escalator allows passengers to enter along the side of the positive triangle and come down from the top. The modern escalator appeared in international exposition held at Paris in 1900.

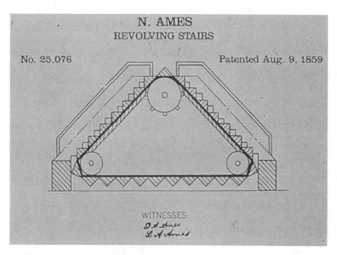

Figure 5.11 Rotary escalator

Now, the escalator is the indispensable transportation facilities for passengers in subway station. Stations with a height difference between of more than 4 to 5 meters will probably need escalators as well-certainly in the up direction. Escalators are expensive, so the number of passengers using the facility must be at a sufficient level to make them worthwhile. As shown in figure 5.12.

5.3.2 Component and Function of Elevator

Escalator is a fixed electric drive device with circular running ladders for transporting passengers up and down. Compared with the lift, escalator can continuously transport passengers and has larger transport capacity. The escalator mainly consists of drive device, balustrade, ladder road, safety system and control system, as shown in table 5.2.

Figure 5.12 Modern escalator

Table 5.2 Component and function of elevator

Structure name	Structural component	Structural function	Pictures
Drive device	Electric motor	Provide power	
	Working brake	Provide the braking force when stopping the operation	
	Decelerator	Reduce running speed	
	Gearing chain	Transfer movement energy	
	Live axle	Transfer of power carrier	
Balustrade	Handrail	Provide armrest	
	Drive device of handrail	Driver handrail	
Step band	Step	People stand	
	Guide rail	Ensure the direction of the step	
	Step chain	Connect the step and deliver the driving force	

Continued

Structure name	Structural component	Structural function	Pictures
Safety system	Host drive chain safety switch	Stop escalator running when the host drive chain is broken or extended	
	Skirt safety device	Stop escalator running when skirt panel is collided	
	Handrail entrance protection switch	Stop escalator running when handrail guard is locked	
	Comb safety device	Stop escalator running when comb safety device is locked	
	Step sagging guard	Stop escalator running when step collapse	
	Unintentional reversal of the direction of travel	Stop escalator running when unintentional reversal of the direction of travel happens	

5.4 Automatic Fare Collection System

5.4.1 Overview of the Automatic Fare Collection System

Automatic Fare Collection System (adhere to AFC) is designed to cut down on the ever-increasing fraud by passengers and staff, more and more high-capacity railway is installing automatic fare collection. AFC has two advantages: It automates the ticket accounting and selling processes and it can give detailed data on system usage. It also reduces ticketless travel, although it never completely eliminates it, and it allows more revenue to be collected without employing an army of staff. The rail transit AFC system is managed and operated by the operating company systematically serving the subway passengers.

The structure of AFC is divided into five parts: ticket, station terminal equipment, station computer system, line central computer system and clearing system. The hierarchical structure is divided according to the fully closed operation mode, based on the contactless IC card as the ticket medium, and according to the respective functions of management, positions of the equipment and the subsystem.

5.4.2 Component and Function of AFC

Hardware and software of AFC mainly consist of automatic gate machine, automatic ticket vending machine, booking office machine, station computer system, etc. Automatic gate machine(abbreviated as AG) is the equipment to realize passengers, passing between the non-paid area and paid area, self-service ticket check in and out of the station by self-service ticket check. As shown in figure 5.13.

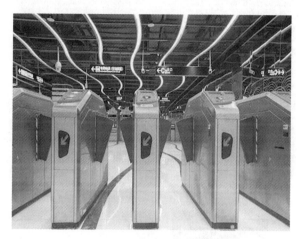

Figure 5.13 AG

Automatic Ticket Vending Machine (abbreviated as TVM), TVM machine is located in the non-paid area of the station, the passengers can buy a ticket for their journey on the TVM. The location of TVMs is important so that they easily seen, easy to access and are not located in place where queues will obstruct the free flow of passenger. TVMs should not be placed close to escalators, stairs or doorway but they should be within sight of the ticket office staff so that problems can be dealt with quickly and easily. As shown in figure 5.14.

Booking office machine (abbreviated as BOM), usually is installed in the sale/supplementary box office or station service center, the stuff using the manual way to complete the ticket processing, ticket sale, ticket analysis, value-adding, refund and other ticket services, so BOM is used as the TVMs and tickets have problems, as shown in figure 5.15.

Station computer system (abbreviated as SC) is an important part of AFC system, and the core part of automatic ticket checking system. SC is the most basic management unit of direct control terminal equipment. Throughout the AFC system, SC is responsible for monitoring and controlling the equipment in the station system automatic setting the start time and end time, operation end time and operation day end time; operators with corresponding authority can set the station system mode or emergency mode and are responsible for passenger flow monitoring, and generate various of report data at the end of operation date; can receive orders and parameters issued by the central computer system and report the system operation, as shown in figure 5.16.

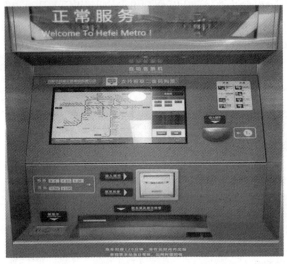

Figure 5.14　TVM

Figure 5.15　BOM

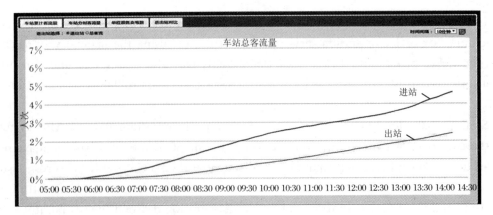

Figure 5.16　Station passenger flow statistics

5.5 Integrated Supervision and Control System

5.5.1 Overview of Integrated Supervision and Control System

Integrated supervision and control system (abbreviated as ISCS) is born to improve efficiency of facilities, ensure the normal operation of equipment and found faulty in time by Continuous Monitoring facilities. In recent years, the manager want to create a system which can connect with all facilities in the station and display the status of facilities on the monitors. ISCS emerged under this background.

In general, the ISCS of urban rail transit connects the different electromechanical equipment system and exchange the date. ISCS can send command and receive condition signal. The system solves the problems of information exchange and resource sharing among various majors in urban rail transit, improves the coordination ability of each system and realizes the efficient linkage mechanism between the systems.

5.5.2 Component and Function of ISCS

As a comprehensive information platform, the ISCS system is designed according to the principles of two-level management (central, station) and three-level control (central, station and local). The functions of the transmission layer and the network layer are realized by Ethernet switch. Each site is connected to the central Ethernet switch via optical fiber to form a large, relatively closed LAN network.

The central ISCS is located in the OCC control center and consists of a variety of equipment. In an emergency, it can make quick decision dissociate the linkage relationship between various devices and quickly respond to emergencies. The ISCS of the station is set in control center of station to realize the supervision and control of all electrical facilities and equipment in the jurisdiction area, so as to improve the safety of the station and create a comfortable and good space for passengers. Local ISCS is located in the seperate room, which is similar to the ISCS of the station. It is not necessary to consider the professional connection with the passenger-related equipment.

ISCS is an integrated system and composes of each integrated subsystem that includes fire alarm system, building automation system, access control system, supervisory control and data acquisition system, etc.

The fire alarm system (abbreviated as FAS) is generally compose of fire detectors, regional alarms and centralized alarms; it can link various fire-extinguishing facilities and communication devices according to the requirements of the project to form the central control system. The FAS system mainly composes of three parts: fire alarm monitoring terminal, fire alarm monitoring network and fire alarm monitoring center, as shown in figure 5.17.

Figure 5.17　Simulation platform of FAS

Building automation system (abbreviated as BAS) integrates computer network, automatic control, communication and distribution intelligent technology to realize the third-party control and management mode of subway environment and equipment system, and comprehensively manage the air conditioning and ventilation, water supply and drainage, lighting, electricity, escalator, safety door and other electromechanical equipment in the subway station and interval tunnel. BAS can also implement the corresponding disaster prevention and blocking mode in the case of fire accidents in underground stations, so that the relevant disaster relief facilities can operate timely and effectively in time according to the design conditions, ensure the safety of passengers and the normal operation of the equipment.

Access control system is a new modern safety management system, which integrates microcomputer automatic identification techniques and modern safety management techniques, it involves electronics, machinery, optics, computer technology, communication technology, biotechnology and many other new technologies. It is an effective measure to manage the entrance and exit of important departments.

Supervisory control and data acquisition system (abbreviated as SCADA) monitor the substation equipment of the whole line, and collect and analyze the operation data of the substation equipment, so as to provide a scientific basis for the scheduling and maintenance of the power supply system. To ensure the safe and economic operation of the traction power supply system, transformer and distribution system.

5.6 Ventilation and Air Conditioning System

5.6.1 Overview of Ventilation and Air Conditioning System

Urban rail transit is a long and narrow underground line, it can be considered that the station of urban rail transit is basically isolated from the ground. There are a lot of heat in the station, which is released by train, facilities and passengers. If the heat isn't timely excluded, the air temperature of internal station will rise. At the same time, the temperature and humidity in the soil around the station can enter the station. If not excluded, it will make passengers unbearable.

Ventilation and air conditioning system refers to improve the environment of the station hall, platform, tunnel, equipment and management room. It can adjust the air temperature and humidity in the specified area and control the concentration of carbon dioxide and harmful dust, ventilation and air conditioning system create a comfortable environment for passengers and staff to meet the requirements of human health and normal operation of related equipment, as shown in figure 5.18.

Figure 5.18 Air pipe

5.6.2 Component and Function of Ventilation and Air Conditioning System

Ventilation and air conditioning system is divide into ventilation system and air conditioning system.

Ventilation system can be divided into tunnel ventilation system, station ventilation system and station smoke exhaustion system. Ventilation facility mainly includes heat exhaust fan, muffler, air processor, air duct, etc. The ventilation system uses fans and related equipments to realize the air flow of the station, provides fresh air for the station, and also realizes the energy exchange between the station and the outside world.

The air conditioning system realizes thermoregulate through refrigeration cycle, cooling water system and chilled water system. Equipments of air conditioning system include compressor, condenser, evaporator, throttle valve, cooling tower, fan coil, fan, water pump, etc. Function of compressor is to compress the normal-temperature refrigerant into a high-temperature and high-pressure refrigerant; the function of condenser is to cool down the high-temperature and high-pressure refrigerant; the evaporator is to exchange cold quantity with external material; the throttle valve is to transform the normal temperature and high pressure refrigerant into a low temperature and low pressure refrigerant.

Refrigeration cycle is that compressor compress the refrigerant and make high temperature and high-pressure refrigerant into condenser; the condenser cools down the refrigerant by moving air or water; the refrigerant will exchange cold quantity with external material in the evaporator and become low temperatures when going through the throttle valve.

The air conditioning system is an important station system to adjust the station temperature, humidity and cleanliness. The air conditioning system mainly provides temperature regulation for the public areas and equipment areas of the station. The station management personnel can control according to the seasonal changes to ensure that the internal environment of the station meets the environmental requirements of the station.

5.7 Writing: How to Write Invitation

(1) **Introduction**

What is an Invitation Letter?

Invitation letters are those letters that are written to invite individuals to a specific event. The main purpose of writing invitation letters is to coordinate the number of guests coming a few days before the date of the event. An invitation letter helps the host handle the event better as they can make arrangements accordingly. We could be written for a conference, a wedding, a graduation ceremony, an exhibition, or an annual day, etc.

(2) **Why are invitations so important?**

In a world that is dominated by instant messaging and APPs like WeChat. But there are some reasons why you should consider investing your time in writing letters to invite people to your party or event.

First impressions are really the last impressions.

If your event is really professional, sending a text message to your guests would hardly be appropriate. You have to send out formal invitation letters to give the perception that your event is extremely professional and has to be taken seriously.

(3) **Composing the letter or email**

You should always start your invitation letter with sentences like:

It is my great pleasure to invite you ...

We're pleased to welcome you ...

Our organization will be venerated to welcome you as a guest ...

It would be a pleasure for us if you could come ...

We would be glad if you could come to ...

On behalf of our organization, we would like to welcome you ...

Writing phrases like these at the beginning of the letter demonstrates your respect and happiness towards inviting an individual to the event.

After you've written that, specify the intent of the event clearly in the first paragraph itself. Mention the most important details like the date, time, and venue in the first paragraph itself. It would be convenient for the recipient to find these important details without reading the entire letter again.

In the second paragraph, You should describe the event's purpose and why you believe it needs to be attended by the recipient.

In addition to all of that, more information can be attached related to the event. For instance, if there is a program for the event, it is better to mention it in the text itself. Additionally, if some special guests or events have been planned for the event, they can be listed in the letter as well.

You can provide additional instructions for the event as some events require special actions from all guests.

That's mostly everything on how to write a perfect main body of an invitation letter. In conclusion, your invitation can contain the following important details:

Reason for the event ...

Venue ...

The date and day on which the event is taking place ...

Time for arrival ...

List of the special programs and events ...

Dear Dr. Richter,

It is my great pleasure to invite you to appear on a panel at the upcoming International Artificial Intelligence Conference. This AI conference will take place on 25 August 2022 in USTC, Hefei, China. We are expecting a packed room, containing some of the most prominent researchers in the field of AI from all over the world, and are eager to end the conference with a panel that summarizes what was new at the conference and points to the future.

The specific topic of the panel is called Machine Learning Reference Architectures. The panelists are Dr. Chen (USTC), Prof. Li (iFlytek Research Institute), Dr. Dre (MIT), Dr. Foster (UOX), etc. There are over 25 expert speakers and industry experts addressing actual trends and best practices. The event allow individuals to present their research to their audience. I hope you will be willing to discuss the work on creating a reference architecture or a set of standards for ML systems.

Unfortunately, due to budget limitations, we are not able to offer any kind of honorarium or reduced registration fee in return for your appearance on the panel. My sincere regrets.

I do hope you will be able to act as a speaker on the panel; your experience and comments will add an important dimension to what is potentially a very important discussion for the field.

Sincerely Yours,

David

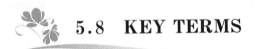

5.8 KEY TERMS

(1) platform screen door (PSD)

(2) automatic sliding door (ASD)

(3) emergency escape door (EED)

(4) door control unit (DCU)

(5) lift

(6) traction system

(7) weight balance system
(8) safety protection system
(9) buffer
(10) overspeed governor
(11) escalator
(12) step
(13) live axle
(14) handrail
(15) automatic fare collection system (AFC)
(16) automatic gate machine (AG)
(17) automatic ticket vending machine (TVM)
(18) booking office machine (BOM)
(19) station computer system (SC)
(20) integrated supervision and control system (ISCS)
(21) operation control center (OCC)
(22) fire alarm system (FAS)
(23) building automation system (BAS)
(24) access control system
(25) supervisory control and data acquisition system
(26) ventilation and air conditioning system
(27) refrigerant
(28) compressor
(29) condenser
(30) evaporator
(31) throttle valve
(32) cooling tower
(33) fan coil
(34) fan
(35) water pump

5.9 EXERCISES

I Match the terms with correct definitions or explanations.

| PSD   lift   elevator   AFC   ISCS   ventilation and air conditioning system |

1. A comprehensive intelligent gating system which integrate architecture, mechanics,

electronic engineering, automation control technology, computer network technology and other disciplines. It is permanently located in the urban rail transit, rail transit, light rail and other rail transit stations. ( )

2. To be used to transport people and goods. ( )

3. A fixed electric drive device with circular running ladders for transporting passengers up or down. ( )

4. Using automatic ticket machine, semi-automatic/ticket machine query machine and other terminal equipment to realize automatic ticket, automatic ticket checking, automatic charge, automatic statistics of closed ticket management through the computer network. ( )

5. To integrate multiple subway electromechanical systems through a unified platform. ( )

6. Adjust the air temperature and humidity in the specified area and control the concentration of carbon dioxide such as harmful dust, which create a comfortable environment for passengers and staff to meet the requirements of human health and normal operation of related equipment. ( )

Ⅱ Answer the following questions according to the text.

1. What is PSD?

2. What is consisted of lift?

3. Can you list of five safety devices?

4. What do the AFC station equipment include?

5. What is the principle of the refrigeration cycle?

Chapter 6 Power and Catenary

There is a wide variety of electric traction systems around the world and these have been built according to the type of railway, its location and the technology available at the time of the installation. Many installations seen today were first built more than 100 years ago, some when electric traction was barely out of its diapers, so to speak, and this has had a great influence on what is seen today.

In the last 20 years there has been a rapid acceleration in railway traction development. This has run in parallel with the development of power electronics and microprocessors. What had been the accepted norms for the industry for sometimes, 80 years, have suddenly been thrown out and replaced by fundamental changes in design, manufacture and operation. Many of these developments are highly technical and complex.

Because the changes have been so rapid, there are still plenty of examples of the original technology around and in regular use. This is useful, since it helps the reader to get to grips with the modern stuff.

6.1 Power Supply

The electric railway needs a power supply that the trains can access at all times. It must be safe, economical and user friendly. It can use either DC (direct current) or AC (alternating current), the former being, for many years, simpler for railway traction purposes, the latter being better over long distances and cheaper to install but, until recently, more complicated to control at train level. In china, it is generally believed that single phase AC is used on main railways, and DC is used in urban transit systems. Figure 6.1 shows the relationship between traction power supply system and power system.

Transmission of power is always along the track by means of an overhead wire or at ground level, using an extra, third rail laid close to the running rails. AC systems always use overhead wires, DC can use either an overhead wire or a third rail, both are common. Both overhead systems require at least one collector attached to the train so it can always be in contact with the power. Overhead current collectors use a "pantograph", so called because that was the shape of most of them until about 30 years ago. The return circuit is via the running rails back to the substation. The running rails are at earth potential and are connected to the substation.

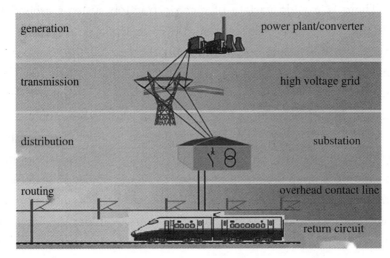

Figure 6.1　Relationship between traction power supply system and power system

6.1.1　AC or DC Traction

It doesn't really matter whether you have AC or DC motors, nowadays either can work with an AC or DC supply. You just need to put the right sort of control system between the supply and the motor and it will work. However, the choice of AC or DC power transmission system along the line is important. Generally, it's a question of what sort of railway you have. It can be summarised simply as AC for long distance and DC for short distance. Of course there are exceptions and we will see some of them later.

It is easier to boost the voltage of AC than that of DC, so it is easier to send more power over transmission lines with AC. This is why national electrical supplies are distributed at up to 765000 volts AC. As AC is easier to transmit over long distances, it is an ideal medium for electric railways. Only the problems of converting it on the train to run DC motors restricted its widespread adoption until the 1960s.

DC, on the other hand was the preferred option for shorter lines, urban systems and tramways. However, it was also used on a number of main line railway systems, and still is in some parts of continental Europe, for example. Apart from only requiring a simple control system for the motors, the smaller size of urban operations meant that trains were usually lighter and needed less power. Of course, it needed a heavier transmission medium, a third rail or a thick wire, to carry the power and it lost a fair amount of voltage as the distance between supply connections increased. This was overcome by placing substations at close intervals — every three or four kilometres at first, nowadays two or three on a 750 volt system — compared with every 20 kilometres or so for a 25 kV AC line.

It should be mentioned at this point that corrosion is always a factor to be considered in electric supply systems, particularly DC systems. The tendency of return currents to wander away from the running rails into the ground can set up electrolysis with water pipes and similar metallics. Schematic diagram of stray current is shown in figure 6.2.

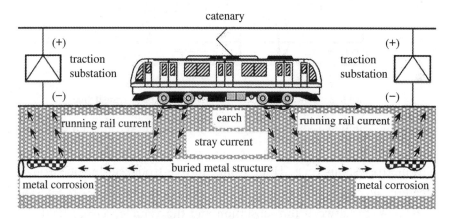

Figure 6.2 Schematic diagram of stray current

This was well understood in the late 19th Century and was one of the reasons why London's Underground railways adopted a fully insulated DC system with a separate negative return rail as well as a positive rail — the four-rail system. Nevertheless, some embarrassing incidents in Asia with disintegrating manhole covers near a metro line as recently as the early 1980s means that the problem still exists and isn't always properly understood. Careful preparation of earthing protection in structures and tunnels is an essential part of the railway design process and is neglected at one's peril.

6.1.2 Distribution

Electric power transmission over long distances is most efficient with high-voltage three-phase AC. For a given power level, higher voltage allows lower current (and therefore lower resistance losses) because the maximum delivered power is the voltage times the current. Thus, for the same conductor cross-section, the voltage drop is lower. Rail transit vehicle on-board equipment typically utilizes 600 V to 1500 V DC picked up from an overhead wire or from a third rail. Propulsion motors may be direct current

(DC) or alternating current (AC). For efficient distribution of power, high-voltage utility power is brought to substations. Transit substations with step-down transformers and rectifier are located at relatively short spacings along the line, as shown in figure 6.3.

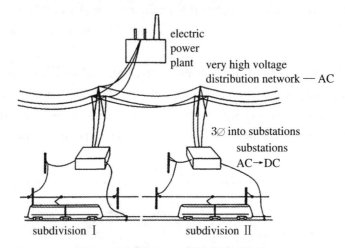

Figure 6.3　Power distribution system of a typical transit line

　　The substations, which reduce voltage and transform AC into DC, allow reduction of the distance that lower voltage DC power travels. To further reduce losses, some recently built metro systems (e.g. Hong Kong) have introduced line operating voltage of 1500 V instead of the customary 600 V to 750 V. The typical voltage drop design criterion allows 30% worst case between the substation and the vehicle. Using 1500 V instead of 750 V halves the current and the voltage drop, while the 30% criterion allows twice the actual voltage difference. The result is that substations can be spaced four times farther apart based purely on distribution voltage considerations. At 750 V, the typical substation spacing on an LRT line is 1.5 km, compared to 6 km possible at 1500 volts. A system with a travel speed of 30 km/h operating with a 15 min headway has trains spaced 7.5 km apart in each direction of travel. With 6 km substation spacing, each substation gets almost steady duty. Conversely, with 1.5 km spacing, each substation would work for about 3 minutes and be idle for 12 minutes during the passage of each train in a given direction.

6.1.3　Return

　　What about the electrical return? There has to be a complete circuit, from the source of the energy out to the consuming item (light bulb, cooking stove or train) and back to the source, so a return conductor is needed for our railway. Simple-use the steel rails the wheels run on. Provided precautions are taken to prevent the voltage getting too high above the zero of the ground, it works very well and has done so for the last century. Of course, as many railways use the running rails for signalling circuits as well, special precautions have to be taken to protect them from interference.

The power circuit on the train is completed by connecting the return to brushes rubbing on the axle ends. The wheels, being steel, take it to the running rails. These are wired into the substation supplying the power and that does the job. The same technique is used for DC or AC overhead line supplies.

 6.2 Overhead Line (Catenary)

Overhead lines or overhead wires are used to transmit electrical energy to trams, trolley buses or trains at a distance from the energy supply point. These overhead lines are known variously as:

Overhead contact system (OCS) — Europe, except UK and Spain.

Overhead line equipment (OLE or OHLE) — UK.

Overhead equipment (OHE) — UK, India, Pakistan and Malaysia.

Overhead wiring (OHW) — Australia.

Catenary — United States, India, UK, Singapore (North East MRT Line), Canada and Spain.

Here, the generic term overhead line is used.

6.2.1 Structure

It is necessary to keep the contact wire to achieve good high-speed current collection, geometry within defined limits. This is usually achieved by supporting the contact wire from above by a second wire known as the messenger wire (US & Canada) or catenary (UK). This wire approximates the natural path of a wire strung between two points, a catenary curve, thus the use of catenary to describe this wire or sometimes the whole system. This wire is attached to the contact wire at regular intervals by vertical wires known as droppers or drop wires. The messenger wire is supported regularly at structures, by a pulley, link, or clamp. The whole system is then subjected to a mechanical tension, as shown in figure 6.4.

As the contact wire makes contact with the pantograph, the carbon surface of the insert on top of the pantograph is worn down. Going around a curve, the "straight" wire between supports will cause the contact wire to cross over the whole surface of the pantograph as the train travels around the curve, causing an even wear and avoiding any notches. On straight track, the contact wire is zigzagged slightly to the left and right of centre at each successive support so that the pantograph wears evenly.

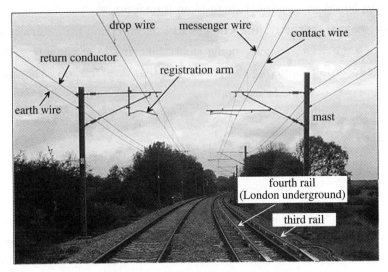

Figure 6.4 The structure of Catenary

The zigzagging of the overhead line is not required for trams using trolley poles or for trolley buses.

Depot areas tend to have only a single wire and are known as simple equipment. When overhead line systems were first conceived, good current collection was possible only at low speeds, using a single wire. To enable higher speeds, two additional types of equipment were developed:

Stitched equipment uses an additional wire at each support structure, terminated on either side of the messenger wire.

Compound equipment uses a second support wire, known as the auxiliary, between the messenger wire and the contact wire. Droppers support the auxiliary from the messenger wire, and additional droppers support the contact wire from the auxiliary. The auxiliary wire can be constructed of a more conductive but less wear-resistant metal, increasing the efficiency of power transmission.

Dropper wires traditionally only provide physical support of the contact wire, and do not join the catenary and contact wires electrically. Contemporary systems use current carrying droppers, which eliminate the need for separate wires.

For tramways there is often just a simple contact wire and no messenger wire. In situations where there is limited clearance to accommodate wire suspensions systems such as in tunnels, the overhead wire may be replaced by rigid overhead rail. This was done when the overhead line had to be raised in the Simplon Tunnel to accommodate taller rail vehicles.

6.2.2 Overhead Contact Wire

The mechanics of power supply wiring is not as simple as it looks (figure 6.4). Hanging a wire over the track, providing it with current and running trains under it is not that easy if it is to do the job properly and last long enough to justify the expense of installing it. The wire must be able to carry the current (several thousand amps), remain in line with the route, withstand wind (in Hong Kong typhoon winds can reach 200 km/h), extreme cold and heat and other hostile weather conditions.

Figure 6.5 Overhead contact wire showing the grooves added to provide for the dropper clips

Overhead catenary systems, called "catenary" from the curve formed by the supporting cable, have a complex geometry, nowadays usually designed by computer. The contact wire has to be held in tension horizontally and pulled laterally to negotiate curves in the track. The contact wire tension will be in the region of 2 tonnes. The wire length is usually from 1000 to 1500 metres long, depending on the temperature ranges. The wire is zigzagged relative to the centre line of the track to even the wear on the train's pantograph as it runs underneath.

The contact wire is grooved to allow a clip to be fixed on the top side (figure 6.5). The clip is used to attach the dropper wire. The tension of the wire is maintained by weights suspended at each end of its length. Each length is overlapped by its neighbour to ensure a smooth passage for the "pan". Incorrect tension, combined with the wrong speed of a train, will cause the pantograph head to start bouncing. An electric arc occurs with each bounce and a pan and wire will soon both become worn through under such conditions.

More than one pantograph on a train can cause a similar problem when the leading pantograph head sets up a wave in the wire and the rear head can't stay in contact. High speeds worsen the problem. The French TGV (high speed train) formation has a power car at each end of the train but only runs with one pantograph raised under the high speed 25 kV AC lines. The rear car is supplied through a 25 kV cable running the length of the train. This would be prohibited in Britain due to the inflexible safety approach there.

A waving wire will cause another problem. It can cause the dropper wires, from which the contact wire is hung, to "kink" and form little loops. The contact wire then becomes too high and aggravates the poor contact.

6.2.3 Subsection and Suspension System

Overhead lines are normally fed in sections like 3rd rail systems, but coverhead sections are usually much longer. Each subsection is isolated from its neighbour by a section insulator in the overhead contact as shown in figure 6.6. Anchor segment joint can also be used in the form of tension compensation by dropping tuo at the lower anchor as shown in figure 6.7. The subsections can be joined through special high speed section switches.

Figure 6.6 Insulated neutral section in an overhead line

To reduce the arcing at a neutral section in the overhead catenary, some systems use track magnets to automatically switch off the power on the train on the approach to the neutral section. A second set of magnets restores the power immediately after the neutral section has been passed.

Various forms of catenary suspension are used depending on the system, its age, its location and the speed of trains using it. Broadly speaking, the higher speeds, the more complex the "stitching", although a simple catenary will usually suffice if the support posts are close enough together on a high speed route. Modern installations often use the simple catenary, slightly sagged to provide a good contact. It has been found to perform well at speeds up to 125 m/hr (200 km/hr).

Figure 6.7　Overhead line suspension system

At the other end of the scale, a tram depot may have just a single wire hung directly from insulated supports. As a pantograph passes along it, the wire can be seen to rise and fall. This is all that is necessary in a slow speed depot environment. I haven't yet mentioned trolley poles as a method of current collection. These were used for current collection on low speed overhead systems and were common on trams or streetcars but they are now obsolete.

DC overhead wires are usually thicker and, in extreme load cases, double wires are used, as in Hong Kong Mass Transit's 1500 V DC supply system. Up to 3000 volts overhead is used by DC main line systems (e.g. parts of France, Belgium and Italy) but below 1500 volts, a third rail can be used. In operating terms, the third rail is awkward because of the greater risk of it being touched at ground level.

It also means that, if trains are stopped and have to be evacuated, the current has to be turned off before passengers can be allowed to wander the track. Third rail routes need special protection to be completely safe.

On the other hand, some people consider the overhead catenary system a visual intrusion. Singapore, for example, has banned its use outside of tunnels.

6.2.4 Transformer Types

On lines equipped with AC overhead wires, special precautions are taken to reduce interference in communications cables. If a communications cable is laid alongside rails carrying the return current of the overhead line supply, it can have unequal voltages induced in it. Over long distances the unequal voltages can represent a safety hazard. To overcome this problem, many systems used booster transformers (figure 6.8 upper drawing). These are positioned on masts at intervals along the route. They are connected to the feeder station by a return conductor cable hung from the masts so that it is roughly the same distance from the track as the overhead line. The return conductor is connected to the running rail at intervals to parallel the return cable and rails. The effect of this arrangement is to reduce the noise levels in the communications cable and ensure the voltages remain at a safe level.

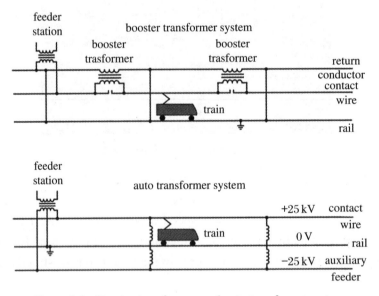

Figure 6.8 Booster transformers and auto transformer system

A more efficient system of AC electrification is known as the auto transformer system (figure 6.8 lower drawing). In effect, it is based on distributing power at 50 kV AC but feeding the power to the trains at 25 kV AC. To achieve this, the supply sub-station transformer is provided with a centre tap secondary winding at 50 kV (set to 55 kV for the maximum limit of contact wire voltage of 27.5 kV). The centre tap is solidly connected to ground so that one terminal is at +25 kV and another at −25 kV. The two supplies at a phase difference of 180 degrees.

With this system, the contact wire is fed at +25 kV and the feeder wire at −25 kV thus the voltage in between these circuits is 50 kV but to ground is 25 kV. The insulation and clearances may still be designed for 25 kV AC only.

6.3 Power Supply Safety

High voltage power supplies must be handled with care. "We use ours carefully, so we'll be fine." "We never had any problems, so we're probably ok."... But, are you sure there is nothing you've neglected or overlooked?

Here show you the correct way to use a high voltage power supply.

6.3.1 To Prevent Discharging

Even for insulators, various discharge phenomena are likely to occur as the applied voltage increases. Therefore, when handling high voltage, it is extremely important to ensure withstand voltage for safety. Withstand voltage is determined by the creepage distance and insulation distance of the insulator, and the shape of the electrode.

Creepage distance: This is the distance along the surface of an insulator between two conductive parts.

Insulation distance: This is the thickness of the insulator when the conductive parts are completely covered by the insulator.

The withstand voltage decreases due to humidity and dirt/dust, and discharge and leakage are more likely to occur as the voltage increases. Choose an appropriate insulating material for the voltage to be used, so that the insulation can be maintained for a long time.

A variety of insulation methods are described in table 6.1.

6.3.2 Handling High Voltage Output Cables

There are a variety of ways to make connections when applying high voltage. Here describe an example method for handling high voltage cables, and precautions that should be observed.

For direct soldering (figure 6.9).

Table 6.1 A variety of insulation methods

Air insulation	When conductive parts are exposed to the air, it has insulation properties of about 500 V/mm under dry conditions. However, these insulation properties are adversely affected by humidity, dust, salt, and hazardous gas, and therefore countermeasures are required. Up to about 3 kV can be routed through air and over printed circuit boards. However, this is suitable only for environments with low humidity and no dust. At 6 kV or more, coronas are likely to occur if there are sharp points, such as solder on conductive parts. Make sure there are no sharp points on conductive parts. At 10 kV or more, coronas are even more likely to occur. Use round electrodes and completely cover the conductive parts with the insulator. At 30 kV or more, discharge tends to occur easily, and therefore measures to reduce the electric field, such as a corona ring, are required.
Gas insulation	SF6 gas is commonly used. It has high dielectric strength and is chemically stable up to a gas temperature of 1800 K. It has a withstand voltage of about 8 kV/mm.
Liquid insulation	Petroleum oils, silicon oils, and fluorinated oils are a few examples of insulation oils.
Solid insulation	If the voltage to be used is 3 kV or less, most resin materials (with high insulation resistance) can be used. At 10 kV or more, Use materials especially high insulation properties. Note that bake lite and phenolic materials will result in large leaks. Epoxy and silicon resins are often used when potting. In some cases only one liquid is used, and in other cases two liquids are mixed together to form the resin. They have a high withstand voltage, and therefore it is possible to shorten the insulation distance.

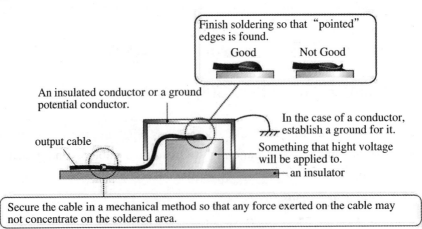

Figure 6.9 An example method for handling high voltage cables

In order to avoid discharging electricity in a manner that will cause bodily harm, either cover the object with an insulator that has sufficient dielectric strength, or cover it with an object that has ground potential so that electricity is not discharged to a different location.

When connecting high voltage cables to create a long high voltage line, it is difficult to keep them connected simply by linking them together, as described above. Therefore, cover the connections with heat-shrink tubing that has dielectric strength. Note that there is a risk of dielectric breakdown in the tube if its withstand voltage is insufficient.

If the insulation withstand voltage of a single tube is not sufficient, use double or triple tubes to ensure sufficient withstand voltage. In addition, if there are rough surfaces on the solder, dielectric breakdown might occur even if the tube has sufficient insulation withstand voltage. Please be sure to make rounded solder joints (figure 6.10).

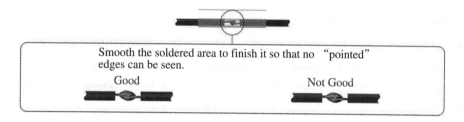

Figure 6.10　An example to make rounded solder joints

6.3.3　Items that Require Particular Attention

When handling high voltage, failure to observe safety precautions can result in electric shock, or even death in the worst case. Be sure to carefully observe the following safety precautions.

(1) **Always Connect a Ground Wire**

In order to avoid discharging electricity in a manner that will cause bodily harm, either cover the object with an insulator that has sufficient dielectric strength, or cover it with an object that has ground potential so that electricity is not discharged to a different location.

(2) **Do Not Touch High Voltage Areas**

When operating equipment, avoid contact with parts that output high voltage as well as high voltage terminals.

Otherwise, electric shock could occur. During normal operation and test operation, extremely high voltage is applied to the terminals. Touching them could lead to a fatal accident.

(3) Overhigh Voltage Areas

With high voltages of 300 V or more, there is a risk of electric shock due to the discharge of electricity even if you do not touch an electrode directly. Either cover electrodes and other high voltage areas with insulators that have sufficient dielectric strength, or cover them with grounded conductive material, to ensure that these areas cannot be touched directly (figure 6.11).

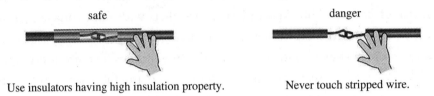

Figure 6.11 An example to cover electrode

(4) Share An Awareness of Danger

Considering the risk of electric shock accidents, if personnel who are experienced in the operation of high voltage power supplies and who know how to perform appropriate first aid measures are not nearby, avoid any contact with high voltage power supplies. In addition, if inexperienced personnel will be operating a high voltage power supply, explain the necessary precautions in advance (such as avoiding contact with hazardous areas) and make sure they completely understand the dangers before allowing them to perform the operations.

(5) Perform Operations with Your Right Hand

In order to reduce the risk of electric current flowing through the important organs of your body even in the event of electric shock, be sure to operate high voltage power supplies with only your right hand while keeping your left hand away from the high voltage power supply and all other equipment.

(6) Turn off the Power before Touching Equipment

Be sure to turn off the power before touching any high voltage areas. Or, make sure that the power has already been turned off. There are capacitors in the output area, which makes it extremely dangerous to touch that area immediately after the power has been turned off. Pay careful attention to the electric charge in these capacitors while connecting them all to ground to discharge the electricity.

(7) Pay Attention to Electric Charge in Cables

The energy that is charged in output shielded cables is discharged by grounding (figure 6.12). However, when the ground is disconnected, in some cases the charge might not have been completely discharged, or the charge might be recovered after some time has passed. Be sure to completely remove all charge from output cables before touching them.

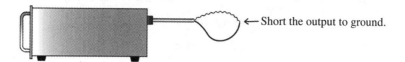

Figure 6.12　Short the output to ground

(8) Disconnect the Input Line before Touching

If you have to touch the inside of the power supply for some reason, follow the instruction manual and turn off the power before disconnecting the input line. And, all the capacitors as well as devices that generated high voltage must be connected to the earth.

In case there is no procedure described in the instruction manual, never remove the cover and do not touch the inside of the power supply.

(9) Instruct Others to Pay Careful Attention

In order to prevent people from entering hazardous areas or inadvertently coming into contact with high voltage areas, clearly mark hazardous areas and instruct others to pay careful attention to the dangers of high voltage (figure 6.13). In addition, when high voltage is generated, issue a warning with a warning lamp or an audible alarm.

Figure 6.13　Warning light and warning sign

6.3.4　Electric Shock

Electric shock, or electrocution, refers to the flow of electric current through the human body. The degree of electric shock is related to the value of the current that flows through the body, and the path through which the current flows. Effects of different currents on human body is shown in table 6.2. While weak currents will produce only a tickling feeling, they could also cause burns, respiratory problems, cardiac impairment, or in the worst case the loss of life.

For a voltage of 100 V, the resistance of human skin is approximately 5 kΩ in dry conditions. In wet conditions, it drops to about 2 kΩ. The resistance of the human body is approximately 300 Ω. If you come into contact with 100 V while your skin is wet, about 22 mA of electric current will flow through your body and you will not be able to break off contact on your own.

Table 6.2 Effects of different currents on human body

Electric current value (mA)	Effect on human body
1	Mild tingling
5	Considerable pain
10	Unbearable pain
20	Intense muscular contraction, unable to break away from circuit on one's own
50	Considerably dangerous
100	Fatal consequences

This is why performing any operations with wet hands is strictly prohibited.

These numerical values are conceptual. If only a weak current flows either because the capacity of the power supply is extremely small or the impedance (similar to resistance) of the circuit is large, the danger will be less. As voltage increases, the air insulation is broken and electricity is discharged, leading to an increased risk of electric shock even if without direct contact with an electrode. Maintain a safe distance from charged areas, as shown in the table 6.3.

Table 6.3 Safe distance

Voltage of charged area (kV)	3	6	10	20	30	60	100	140	270
Safe distance (cm)	15	15	20	30	45	75	115	160	300

Care must be taken to avoid approaching these charged areas.

6.3.5 First Aid for Electric Shock

(1) Rescue

Immediately move the victim away from the conductor through which the electric current is flowing. At that time, avoid direct contact with both the conductor through which the electric current is flowing and the body of the victim, to avoid becoming subject to electric shock yourself. Immediately turn off the high voltage power supply and ground the circuit. If the high voltage power supply cannot be turned off, either ground the circuit or use an axe with a dry wooden handle to cut the input and output cables. In that case, take care that electric sparks are not discharged from the cables. If it is not possible to either turn off or ground the circuit, use an insulator such as a dry board or clothing to rescue the victim. Call an ambulance immediately.

(2) Symptoms

Do not confuse the symptoms of electric shock with death. In addition to severe burns, the symptoms of electric shock also include unconsciousness, respiratory arrest, cardiopulmonary arrest, paleness, and rigidity.

(3) Treatment

① If the victim is not breathing properly, immediately start artificial respiration on the spot. Note that the victim should be moved to a safe location only if the lives of the victim or rescuers are in danger by remaining at the accident site.

② If you start artificial respiration, continue performing artificial respiration correctly either until the victim begins breathing again on their own, or until medical professionals are able to take over.

③ If there is another person available to perform artificial respiration with you in alternating turns, do so continuously without interrupting the rhythm. Electric shock might also cause burns inside the body, which can lead to serious consequences if left untreated.

Therefore, in addition to first aid, be sure to have the victim examined by a physician as soon as possible.

Although here have described the measures that should be taken in the event an accident occurs, it goes without saying that the best action is to prevent accidents from occurring in the first place. Please develop a thorough understanding of the dangers of high voltage, and use high voltage power supplies both safely and correctly in order to ensure that electric shock accidents never happen.

6.4 Writing: How to Write An Email Requesting Something

There are many times when we need something. It can be leave from your boss, an interview at a new company, business advice from an expert, or even a recommendation. It can be daunting to write request emails that will get the recipient to grant your request. In this part, we will show you how to write an email requesting something and actually get a response!

(1) What Is a Request Email?

As the name suggests, a request email is an email you write, asking for something, whether information, favor, or service. The email can be to ask for help, authorization, advice, support, etc. It can also be an appeal or inquiry. Since it's a request, the email should be very polite, precise, brief, and specific. The recipient should be able to know what you want by the end of the email.

(2) Preparation for Writing A Request Email

① Focus on the "you" perspective. When requesting something from the recipient, it can be tempting to sink into talking about yourself. The secret is to make it about the recipient. Tell them how you appreciate what they have been doing. Let them know you are a big fan of their work and how their work has transformed your life before asking for an interview. The "you first" approach will help you get backstage passes, several leaves a year, interviews and recommendation letters with minimal effort. Remember, focus on them!

② Sell your benefits. What value are you adding to the recipient so that you should secure an interview? If you ask for a favor, an internship, or just an interview, ensure you have done thorough research on the pain points and how you can provide solutions. Set yourself apart!

③ Make it impossible to say no. How? Anticipate rejection and come up with a solution to their reasons for saying no. For instance, if you want to be an intern for the best-selling writer, they may say no because they don't have a budget for your salary. Offer to intern for free. You will be making it impossible to say no.

(3) Structure

The structure of a request email is similar to that of an official letter. Keep it formal and respectful to increase the chances of the person doing what you are asking.

① Subject line. The subject line should state why you are emailing the person. It will determine whether the recipient opens your email or not. Keep it short but precise. For instance, "requesting a recommendation letter".

② Salutation/ email introduction. The salutation should be formal unless you know the recipient personally. If you know the name of the recipient, use it to create a personal feeling. For instance, "hello Josh" is likely to make the recipient open the email than "hello sir".

③ Body. The body of a request is very simple to craft. Just remember the acronym rap, which stands for reference, action, and polite close. In reference, let the recipient know why you are writing. For instance, "I am writing to request a recommendation for my internship at company. The recipient does not have to read through the whole email to know what you want. Ensure you are using polite language. You can start off with phrases like:

I am writing to request ...

With reference to ...

I am writing in response to your inquiry ...

Under action, clearly state what you want the recipient to do for you. For instance, "please send the documents before evening for compiling". the action should also be very polite because it's a request. Remember, you are not entitled to what you are requesting. Also, keep it brief and straight to the point. A long body is likely to discourage the recipient from reading the email.

Finish by thanking the recipient for the time spent reading the email. You can use polite phrases like:

Thanks in advance for your assistance.

Please let me know if you have any questions.

I look forward to hearing from you.

Please let me know when you are available.

④ Email ending. The email end also creates an impression, so ensure you keep it as professional and precise as the rest of the email. Keep it simple, for instance:

Best regards,

[name]

(4) Email Do's and Don'ts

Email do's:

- Be precise.

Nobody wants to read a novel, especially when you are writing to them, taking up their time and requesting something from them. No need for beating around the bush. Keep it short and precise!

- Limit your email to one request.

You may want a thousand things, but don't confuse the recipient. You will end up burying the most important request or even getting nothing out of it!

- Use a polite tone and language.

A request email should be very polite, like someone who is asking for something and not demanding. Remember that the recipient owes you nothing. Once you are done writing, try reading it from the recipient's perspective. Would you grant a request to the writer based on the tone?

- Proofread your email.

You don't want your recipient to be put off by poor grammar or punctuation. Ensure you have proof read your email. You can make sure that your email is clear and free of mistakes by using a writing tool such as Grammarly. This will greatly increase your chances of success when making your request.

Email don'ts:

- Don't write anything inappropriate in the email. Remember, emails are not private.

- Don't forget to proofread. It does not matter if you are in a hurry. Poor grammar is a turn-off.

• Don't send an email if it can be addressed in person or over the call. People have too many emails every day. They don't want more!

(5) **Email Samples**

Are you still having trouble writing an email to ask for something? We got you! Here are some samples you can customize to suit your needs.

Sample 1: Leave request email

> Subject line: Request for one week leave
> Dear [name]:
>   With reference to our meeting in the afternoon, I would like to request a one week leave. I have been following up with the interns, and I am feeling a bit under the weather due to working late.
>   I have been monitoring my health for 10 days, but there has been no improvement, I would like to take time off to see a doctor and get back on my feet to do a better job. I have ensured that all tasks I cannot handle online will be attended to by [name of colleague] so everything can run smoothly in the department.
>   I will be awaiting your response. Thanks in advance.
> Sincerely,
> [name]

Sample 2: Letter of recommendation request email

> Subject: Requesting a recommendation letter
> Dear Professor [name]:
>   I am writing to request a recommendation letter as I apply for an internship at [company name]. As you may know, I am graduating end of September and need to have completed my internship.
>   As my professor, I know that your recommendation will go a long way in helping me secure an internship and maybe even a job in the future. Your recommendation will add a lot of weight to my application.
>   I await your response. Thank you in advance for the consideration and continued support in my studies.
> Best regards,
> [name]

6.5 KEY TERMS

(1) power supply
(2) traction substation
(3) direct current (DC)
(4) alternating current (AC)
(5) overhead systems
(6) collector
(7) pantograph
(8) return circuit
(9) transmission
(10) transformer
(11) distribution
(12) corrosion
(13) stray current
(14) negative return rail
(15) positive rail
(16) voltage drop
(17) overhead line
(18) overhead contact system (OCS)
(19) overhead line equipment (OLE or OHLE)
(20) overhead equipment (OHE)
(21) overhead wiring
(22) catenary
(23) catenary system
(24) contact wire
(25) drop wire
(26) messenger wire
(27) registration arm
(28) mast
(29) return conductor
(30) earch wire
(31) stitched equipment
(32) compound equipment
(33) subsection

(34) section switch
(35) insulator
(36) suspension system
(37) creepage distance
(38) insulation distance

6.6 EXERCISES

I Match the terms with correct definitions or explanations.

| catenary system   stray current   substation   transformer |
| power supply   catenary   creepage distance |

1. An overhead wire from which a transit vehicle collects propulsion and auxiliary power.   (   )

2. That form of electric contact system in which the overhead contact wire is supported from one or more longitudinal wires or cables (messengers), either directly by hangers or by hangers in combination with auxiliary conductors and clamps.   (   )

3. Electric currents which are not a part of the system, that may affect a signaling system or contribute to galvanic corrosion.   (   )

4. A unit that supplies electrical energy and maintains constant voltage and/or current output within in specific limits.   (   )

5. The shortest distance between two conducting parts measured along the surface or joints of the insulating material between them.   (   )

6. A place where the strength of electric power from a power station is reduced before it is passed on to homes and businesses.   (   )

7. A device for reducing or increasing the voltage of an electric power supply, usually to allow a particular piece of electrical equipment to be used.   (   )

II Answer the following questions according to the text.
1. Draw the traction power supply circuit and mark the power transmission direction and

equipment.

2. Draw the schematic diagram of OCS and mark the equipment.

3. Describe the typical power supply mode of rail transit.

4. Discuss the development trend and key technologies of traction power supply.

Chapter 7 Telcom System

The urban rail transit communication system is an important means of commanding train operation, highway communication, transmitting various information and improving transportation efficiency. The communication system should also complete the traffic scheduling together with the signal system, and provide an information transmission channel for the signal system. In the event of fire and other accidents, the communication system is also the main means of emergency response, rescue and disaster relief. Through the study of this project, master the main functions of the communication system. Learn about common mediums of communication. Further expand professional vocabulary and memorize professional vocabulary related to communication system.

7.1 Structure of Telcom System

Urban rail transit communication system is mainly composed of telecommunication transmission system, telephone system (including public official telephone system, inner station and line-side telephone system), CCTV supervision system, wireless dispatching communication system, broadcasting system, clock system, etc. The following is a brief introduction of each component system. The whole system forms the comprehensive communication network for service use, sending all kinds of information like pictures, voice, video, data, words and so on. It is not only an important means to conduct the operation of the subway but also it can serve the purpose of preventing disasters, providing aids and dealing with accidents under abnormal circumstances.

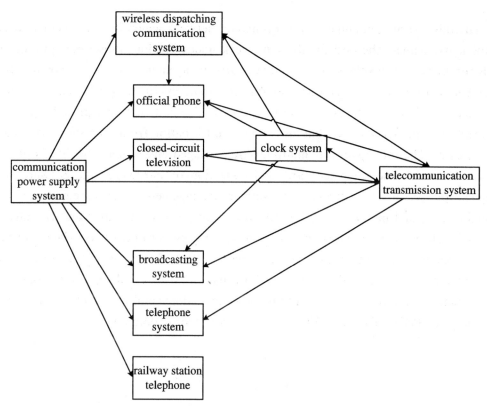

Figure 7.1 The components of the urban rail transit communication system

 ## 7.2 Function of Subsystem

In order to ensure the safe, reliable, punctual, high-density and high-efficiency operation of trains in the urban rail transit system, and to realize the centralized and unified command of transportation and the automation of train scheduling, the urban rail transit system must be equipped with a dedicated, complete and independent communication system. Connection all functional departments of the urban rail transit system through the traffic dispatching system.

Some functions of subsystems list briefly as following.

7.2.1 The Transmission System

It is the basic of the telecommunication system. It can provide the technological departments within the subway system with reliable and flexible data-transmitting channels.

The rail transit communication transmission network generally consists of four basic components, namely the optical fiber, network nodes, various subscriber line interface cards for users to access the system, and network management system, as shown in figure 7.2. A network node is a necessary way for users to access the network. Various types of subscriber line interface cards connect with nodes. The node not only provides power for subscriber line interface cards, but also receives information from each subscriber line interface card. The information is multiplexed, packaged and sent to the fiber optic network. Subscriber line interface card is a collection of hardware and software which designed for users to access the system. Network management systems are generally based on mainstream and mature operating systems, with powerful features and friendly user interface. Through the network management system, users can easily configure, expand, manage and maintain the transmission network. With fiber optic as its transmission media and optical wave as the carrier of information, it can realize a large volume and long-distance transmission. The transmission system adopts multiple kinds of transmission technology of PDH, SDH and ATM to send voice, word, data and pictures.

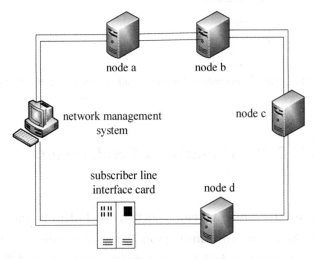

Figure 7.2 The communication transmission

The communication transmission system is the main means of connecting the train dispatching command center and the station. It is also the main means of information transmission between the station and the station, and is the basis for the establishment of the rail transit communication network.

7.2.2 The Wireless Telecommunication System

The dedicated wireless communication system provides a reliable means of communication between fixed users and mobile users of the project. It provides important guarantees for driving safety, improving transportation efficiency and management level, improving service quality, and responding to emergencies. According to the actual situation of rail communication operation and management, the general wireless communication system is divided into the following subsystems:

(1) Train Dispatching Subsystem

The train dispatching subsystem is used for communication among train dispatchers, train drivers, station attendants, and platform attendants to meet traffic requirements.

(2) Maintenance Dispatching Subsystem

The maintenance dispatching subsystem is used for communication between the maintenance dispatcher and the on-site attendants to meet the daily maintenance and emergency repair requirements of lines and equipment.

(3) Disaster Prevention and Environmental Control Dispatching Subsystem

Disaster prevention and environmental control dispatching subsystem is used for communication among disaster prevention and environmental control dispatchers, station attendants, on-site commanders and related personnel to meet the needs of accident rescue and disaster prevention.

(4) Depot/Parking Lot Dispatching Subsystem

The depot/parking lot dispatching subsystem is used for communication among the depot/parking signal building attendants, train inspection depot operation attendants, train drivers, and on-site operators to meet the needs of shunting and vehicle maintenance within the depot.

The wireless trunking system of urban rail transit often adopts the trunking system of multi-base station and multi-zone system with some additional connection, signal relay and amplification equipment (such as radio frequency/optical fiber repeater) to form a wired and wireless network. The central equipment and the base station are connected by a wired channel, and the base station is transmitted through the signal distribution equipment, using leaky cables or antenna radiation to realize the wireless connection with the mobile station, as shown in figure 7.3.

7.2.3 Telephone System

(1) Official Phone

The official phone system is an important system that provides safe, reliable and high-speed communication for train operation, dispatching, disaster prevention and alarm. Therefore, the system must be designed to be fast and non-blocking. When an emergency occurs, it can be quickly turned into a command control communication system for disaster prevention, rescue and accident handling. As a result, it adopts the private network.

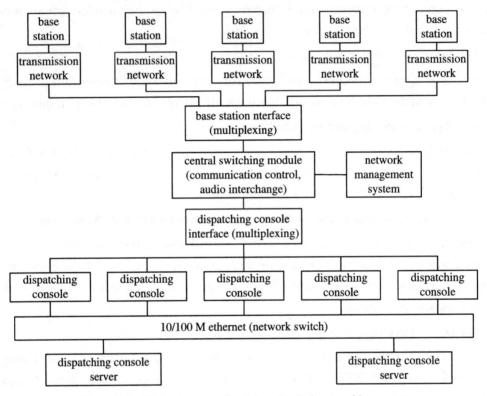

Figure 7.3　Dial-up access of rail transit wireless trunking system

In figure 7.4, the official telephone is composed of three user program-controlled switchers through the transmission system in a loop network. Its advantage is that when the line between any two switches is interrupted, the call can still be maintained through the circuitous transmission line to ensure the reliability of the network.

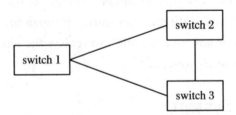

Figure 7.4　Loop network structure

(2) Special Purpose Telephone

The special purpose telephone system is composed of four parts: traffic control telephone, inner station telephone system, telephones for blocking and wayside telephone.

(3) Traffic Control Telephones

Traffic control telephones (figure 7.5) are installed for communications between division or subdivision train controller and the operator at stations and other divisions or subdivisions to direct the movements of trains and to organize station operations.

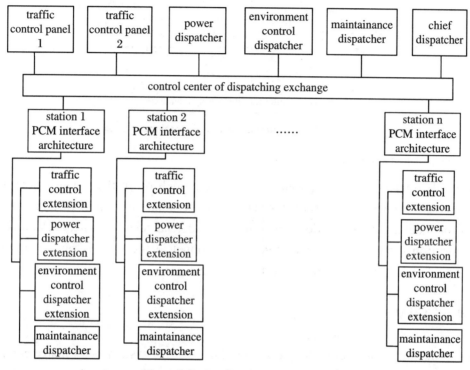

Figure 7.5 Traffic control telephones

Only one pair of wires is required to link up all stations and other division or subdivision offices with the traffic control office. In other words, traffic control telephones link up all the above mentioned units with the same traffic control section.

The exchange of traffic control is located in the traffic control office and extension sets for traffic control are installed at every station and other offices concerned. When the train controller wants to call out of a station, he just presses the calling button on the calling and talking facility to send out an audio-frequency code which rings the bell of the extension at the desired station. Operators at stations may call the train controller directly through his extension as the controller hears the call from loudspeaker.

(4) Inner Station Dispatching Telephone

Such telephones provide communications between the shunting controller and other outdoor workers related to shunting movements (figure 7.6).

(5) Telephones for Blocking

Telephones for blocking provide communications between adjacent stations for the blocking of section. The block machines for all relay semi-automatic system are equipped with such telephone.

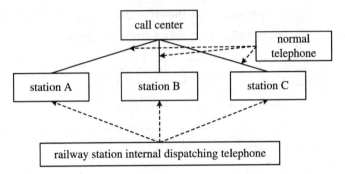

Figure 7.6　Railway station internal dispatching telephones

(6) Wayside Telephone

Wayside telephone are telephones installed in tunnels or on the ground, next to elevated lines. It connects the dispatcher station of the adjacent station through the telephones for blocking in the station, or join in the official telephone network to provide communication services for the maintenance personnel in the tunnel, on the ground or beside the elevated line, and the train driver in emergency.

7.2.4 CCTV

In urban rail transit, closed-circuit television (CCTV) system as an image communication system, can realize intuitive real-time dynamic image monitoring, recording and tracking control, and so on. Provide real-time image information of main areas such as station halls, platforms, entrances and exits, computer rooms, train inspection warehouses, and yards of the stations under their monitor for the dispatcher of the control center, the station/depot attendants, train drivers and platform staff. Monitor train operation, passenger flow, passengers getting on and off, and so on. When a disaster occurs, it can be used as an important command tool for disaster prevention and dispatch; at the same time, it provides important visual information for station passenger evacuation and social security.

The closed-circuit television system is an important means to ensure the organization and safety of urban rail transit traffic, and an auxiliary communication tool to improve the transparency of traffic command. Its main functions are shown in the following aspects.

Provide the first-level traffic management personnel (traffic dispatcher, environmental control dispatcher, public security duty officer, duty supervisor and so on) of the dispatch center with image information of the traffic conditions in each platform area and the flow of passengers in the station hall.

Provide on-site real-time image information of train stops, starting, door opening and closing, ticket vending machines, gate entrances and exits to the station attendents.

7.2.5 Broadcasting System

The broadcasting system in the urban rail transit system can be divided into two parts according to the installation location of the equipment. One is terrestrial broadcasting, and the other is vehicle broadcasting. The role of broadcasting system is not only to inform the staff of timely releasing traffic related information, and making the staff work in concert, but also to notify passengers of vehicle arrival, departure or line transfer, also play music so that passengers will enjoy more convenient and comfortable condition. When disasters occur, it can be used to evacuate passengers.

(1) The Terrestrial Broadcasting System

The terrestrial broadcasting system generally consists of station broadcasting system equipment, control center broadcasting equipment and transmission lines, as shown in figure 7.7.

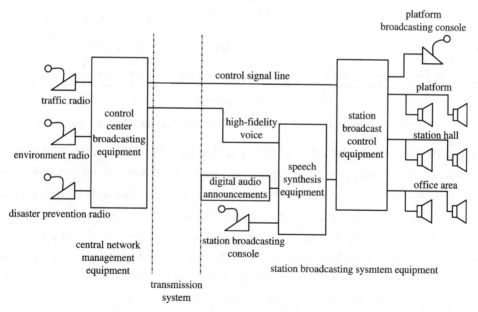

Figure 7.7 The terrestrial broadcasting system

The urban rail transit broadcasting system adopts broadcasting method of multi-sound source selection, that is, different areas can simultaneously select the parallel broadcasting function of different sound source broadcasting, and the sound source can be selected from microphone input, line, pre-stored voice, etc. One is to inform passengers of vehicle arrival, departure, line transfer, schedule change, vehicle delay, safety and other information, or play music so that passengers will enjoy more convenient and comfortable conditions. It is used by the staff in charge of dispatching at the control center and the persons on duty at the stations so that they can provide the passengers with the information of the operation of trains, safety and guidance and send orders and notices to the working staff. When disasters occur, it can be used to evacuate passengers.

(2) On-board Broadcasting System

There are two modes of on-board broadcasting system, one is designed for trains running on the ground, and the other is designed for vehicles running in tunnels.

① On-board broadcasting system for vehicles running on the ground.

As the vehicle is running on the ground, the GPS positioning signal can be received on the vehicle. The on-board broadcast is generally triggered by GPS receiver. The system has realized automatic broadcast mode, as shown in figure 7.8. The system equipment consists of GPS receiver, control equipment for vehicle broadcasting and loudspeaker.

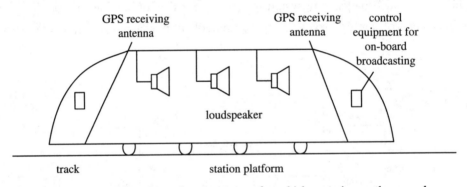

Figure 7.8 On-board broadcasting system for vehicles running on the ground

The GPS receiver receives the satellite positioning signal and transmits the signal to the broadcast control equipment to realize the function of vehicle information positioning. The on-board broadcast control equipment receives the vehicle positioning signal of the GPS receiver, judges the content of the broadcast information, and broadcast the stored information. It also has the function of manual broadcasting. When it is necessary to broadcast emergency information or the GPS receiver fails, the driver can manually broadcast the information through the control buttons on the control panel. Then the loudspeaker system can broadcast to the passengers on the vehicle.

② On-board broadcasting system for vehicles running in tunnels.

Generally, vehicles traveling in tunnels cannot receive GPS positioning information, and need to trigger the device through the track circuit to realize the function of automatic broadcast information. The structure of the on-board broadcast system for vehicles running in tunnels is shown in figure 7.9, The system equipment consists of track circuit triggering equipment, on-board receiving equipment, on-board broadcast control equipment, and loudspeaker.

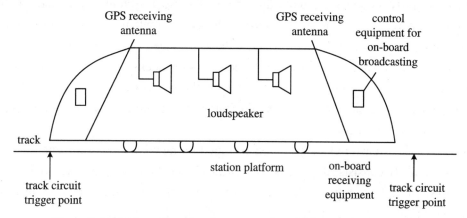

Figure 7.9 On-board broadcasting system for vehicles running in tunnels

The track circuit trigger device is installed on the track that needs to be broadcast when the vehicle enters and leaves the station, and sends position information to the on-board receiving device. After the on-board receiving device receives the information, it transmits the signal to the on-board broadcast control device. The vehicle-mounted broadcast control equipment receives the location information of the vehicle-mounted receiving equipment, and judges the content of the broadcast information. Other functions are the same as the ground vehicle-mounted broadcast control equipment.

7.2.6 The Clock System

The clock system is one of the important components of the urban rail transit operation. It provides a unified standard time for staff, passengers and other related systems, so that the timing equipment of each system can be synchronized with the system. In order to achieve a unified time standard, the clock system provides synchronous clock signal for communication equipment, so that each communication node equipment can run synchronously. The system generally uses the global positioning system (GPS) to mark time information.

(1) Composition of Urban Rail Transit Clock System

The clock system consists of a central primary master clock, a monitoring terminal, a secondary master clock and a slave clock, as shown in figure 7.10. In the figure, SCADA is used to represent supervisory control and data acquisition system, and FAS is used to represent the fire alarm system.

The GPS standard clock signal receiving unit is generally located in the control center, receives satellite time, and provides synchronous clock source signals to the main and backup master clocks of the central primary master clock.

The primary master clock is generally located in the control center and consists of a clock system host, a conversion unit, and so on. The clock system host includes a display unit, a main master clock, a backup master clock, an input interface, and so on. The conversion unit detects the working state of the main master clock and realizes the automatic conversion between the main and backup master clocks.

The monitoring equipment is also located in the control center and is connected to the primary master clock, which can monitor the running status of the main equipment of the clock system in real time.

The secondary master clock system is installed in the communication equipment room of each station. It consists of a clock system host and a conversion unit. It is an independent system that can receive the standard time information and command information sent by the primary master clock, it can also control the operation of the slave clocks, and can also operate independently of the central master clock.

The slave clock is installed in the station hall, platform, duty office, control center dispatch room and other places where time information needs to be displayed.

(2) **Networking Mode of Urban Rail Transit Clock System**

In order to ensure the safe, punctual and reliable operation of urban rail transit system, close cooperation is required between various departments. The urban rail transit clock system has the following two networking modes:

① Clock system separate networking mode.

The clock system in urban rail transit generally adopts the control center/station two-level networking method. As mentioned above, the primary master clock receives the standard time signal from GPS, corrects its own crystal oscillator, generates a stable standard time signal, and transmits it to the secondary master clock in stations and parking lots through the transmission system.

The secondary master clock receives the standard time signal of the primary master clock, corrects its own crystal oscillator, generates a stable standard time signal, drives all the slave clocks it carries, displays the unified time, and provides unified time for passengers and staff.

The primary master clock also provides a unified time signal for other systems in the control center, so that the timing equipment of each system is synchronized with the clock system.

② Hybrid networking mode of clock system and passenger guidance system.

The main function of the passenger guidance system is to provide passengers with information about train arrivals and departures through text, images and sounds. It can guide passengers to take the train quickly and conveniently, also provide news, advertisements, entertainment information services. Display terminals are generally located in the halls and platforms of each station.

Considering the content and interface of the two systems, the clock system can be integrated with the passenger guidance system. The specific network mode is to retain the master clocks at all levels at each station, and cancel the slave clocks in the station hall and platform. The primary master clock provides the time signal for the passenger guidance system in the control center or the secondary master clock directly provides the time signal to the passenger guidance equipment of the station. The passenger guidance system displays the clock information in the fixed windows on the display terminals of the station halls and platforms, as shown in figure 7.10.

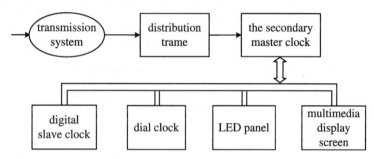

Figure 7.10 Hybrid networking mode of clock system and passenger guidance system

Both of the above two clock system networking modes can meet the needs of urban rail transit operation. In the first scheme, each system operates independently without affecting each other. The second scheme uses the passenger guidance system to display the time information and completes the display of the slave clock. The display screen does not have the function of its own time correction. When the clock system fails or the line fails, the clock information cannot be displayed on the screen. However, it has the characteristics of economy, rationality and high degree of integration.

7.3 Writing: Introduction to Notice

There are several different definitions listed under the diction of notice. Under the situation of applied writing, notice means a formal announcement or notification of something.

The constituents of a notice (title; body: event, time, place, participants, ways of participation, cautions; signature: notice issuer and date).

Sample: A notice of meeting

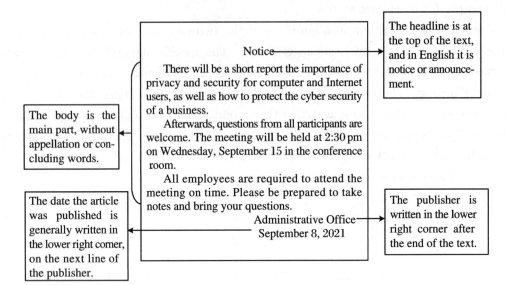

图 7.11

7.4 KEY TERMS

(1) pseudo-synchronous digital hierarchy (PDH)

(2) synchronous digital hierarchy (SDH)

(3) asynchronous transfer mode (ATM)

(4) digital audio announcements

(5) closed circuit television (CCTV) supervision system

(6) traffic dispatching system

(7) optical fiber

(8) public official telephone system

(9) inner station telephone system

(10) line-side telephone system

(11) the wireless trunking system

(12) leaky cable

(13) dial-up access

(14) program-controlled

(15) train borne

(16) wayside equipment

(17) the global positioning system (GPS)

(18) the fire alarm system (FAS)

(19) supervisory control and data acquisition (SCADA)
(20) traffic control telephone

7.5 EXERCISES

I Match the terms with correct definitions or explanations.

| SCADA   inner station telephone   dispatch point   dial-up access   CCTV |
| supervision system |

1. Supervisory control and data acquisition, it measures flow, temperature, pressure and other parameters through sensors at key points along the pipeline and sends the data to a central control center. ( )

2. Providing communications between the shunting controller and other outdoor workers related to shunting movements. ( )

3. The location at which operating employees receive their assignments or the location at which trips are started or restarted. ( )

4. The data communication network is connected by using a public switching communication network. ( )

5. A television system that is not used for broadcasting but is connected by cables to designated monitors (as in a factory or theater). ( )

II Answer the following questions according to the text.

1. What does the telecommunication system consist of?

2. Can you list the function of the telecommunication system according to your urban rail transit?

3. Which kind of communication medium is used?

Chapter 8 Monorail

Monorails encompass many different transit systems with the common feature that their vehicles ride on or are suspended from a single rail or beam. The first monorail was opened in Wuppertal, Germany, in 1901. Called "Hovering Railway", it was built along a narrow valley of the river Wupper, which is the "spine" of the city. Suspended mostly over the river, it actually represents the only true "monorail" in the world: its cars are spended from a single rail built underneath a supporting steel frame. The cars hang on wheels which are driven by multiple electric motors operating at 750 volts DC, fed from a live rail below the running rail. It has had a very safe and reliable operation and enjoys great popularity due to its unique design and scenic visibility. In recent decades, some reconstructed sections of the line have been built with a concrete structure to reduce the noise produced by the old steel structures. Articulated 6-wheel vehicles have been introduced to replace the old 4-wheel rolling stock.

From their early appearance, monorail systems have acquired an image of the "transit of the future", being shown dashing as a hanging train or riding on a narrow beam above urban streets. This latter type, straddling on a concrete beam, is the monorail system developed by the Swedish industrialist Axel Wenner Gren in the 1950s and named Alweg. That model, with subsequent improvements and modifications, is now the most common type among the several dozen monorails operating in the world. Most monorails are in Japan, but some are also operated in the United States and other countries.

8.1 Types of Monorail

There are two basic types of monorails:

Supported (straddling) monorails running on a concrete beam with two trucks, each with four supporting and eight guiding rubber tires running along six surfaces along the beam. The vehicle body is above the wheels, in some models with wheel boxes placed under the supporting wheels in the passenger compartment. Long side skirts cover the guiding wheels.

Suspended monorails hang from a guide beam, which may be a single rail or an enclosed tube with four running surfaces, two for supporting and two for guiding wheels. Thus the trucks run along protected surfaces inside the beam and carry the vehicle body, which is suspended through a slot in the beam, as shown in figure 8.1.

Figure 8.1 A suspended monorail in Germany

All monorails consist of one or, most often, three-to six-car TUs and have exclusive ROW, so that they functionally belong in the rapid transit category of modes. One of the most heavily used monorail lines in the world, which has six-car trains, while the most recently opened monorail in the United States, the Bombardier-built line in Las Vegas, operates four-car trains. Operating with headway of 2 to 3 min, monorails can have capacities similar to those of moderate-sized RRT systems. A suspended monorail in Japan is shown in figure 8.2.

With ROW consisting of a single beam, supported monorails have a small, unobtrusive infrastructure with a considerably smaller profile and shadow than conventional rail aerial lines. The single guideway, however, requires to the roof than rail vehicles. With a much higher total vehicle profile, monorails are not suited to tunnel alignments. The aerial alignments are a part of their attraction and visibility in the city, but the acceptability of trains traveling between tall buildings is lower than is often imagined. Objections to trains taking air space and passing by windows of buildings are not much less than those to aerial alignments for rail systems. With respect to stations, monorail has very similar requirements to rail, so that they face the same problems in fitting their elevated stations in center city areas.

Figure 8.2 A suspended monorail in Japan

Rubber-tire support gives monorails advantages over rail vehicles in negotiating steeper grades and curves. The Haneda Airport Line in Tokyo demonstrates how monorail guide ways can better follow various constrained alignments.

Mechanically, monorail guideway switches consist of a movable beam, which is much more complicated, slower, and requires larger space than rail switches. Crossing of guideways is even more complex, so that any guideway layout with switches and multiple beams, such as larger stations and yards, are very complex and require large areas. This is one of the reasons that all monorail installations consist of single lines only; there are no monorail networks of several lines anywhere in the world.

In summary, monorails can operate efficiently and be acceptable to urban environment on single lines in wide boulevards, green areas or along bodies of water, utilizing aerial structures. They are not suited to tunnel or surface alignments, to urban streets with tall buildings, or for networks of more than single lines. Thus, monorails can be used efficiently as APM systems in open areas and in tourist areas where their exotic appeal is an asset.

Planning and discussions about monorails are often controversial because there is a considerable difference between their popular appeal and rational engineering analysis and comparison of their features with those of conventional rail modes. The latter are almost never favorable for monorails, so that their applications are mostly found in areas with special character and tourist appeal.

The difference between emotional support and engineering/economic system evaluation of monorails has been demonstrated by the developments in Seattle during the 2000 ~2005 period. A transit planning process and several popular referenda for its financing during the 1990s led to the adoption of a plan for construction of a long light rail line as well as improved bus and regional rail services. Influenced by the propaganda against rail transit produced in most U.S. cities, the promoters of monorails claimed that a monorail network would be a more effective and attractive mode for Seattle, which has operated one shuttle monorail line built for the World's Fair in 1962. The grass-roots movement resulted in two popular referenda that proposed construction of a 14-km-long monorail line and sources for financing it, both totally unrelated to the already adopted transit plan for the region. The claims were brought up that with its aerial alignment, monorail would be easier to build than a partially tunneled LRT line and that it would be more attractive for the city's central area.

As the planning proceeded, however, design difficulties proved to be much greater than foreseen. Aerial structures and stations in city streets with tall buildings, large stations, and other installations were criticized and their redesign escalated the costs. To keep the costs moderate, construction of a single-beam section was considered — a feature not suitable for a busy transit line that needs reliable operation with short headway, which is particularly inconvenient for monorail's switching characteristics. Following many efforts to manage the required financing, a plan was developed for the sale of bonds, which would be repaid over 40 years for a total cost of about $11 billion. This plan caused a political uproar and a call for another referendum, at which the entire plan was rejected. This case demonstrates the mentioned differences between popular support for monorails and factual planning — that is, technical and financial analyses of that mode.

The failure in Seattle does not mean that monorails have no future in urban transportation. They will continue to have a certain appeal and it is likely that monorails of different designs will be used for special applications, such as certain APM services (airports, amusement parks, shuttles in major activity centers) and in tourist-oriented cities.

8.2 Overview of Chongqing Monorail

A route map of Chongqing Monorail No. 2 Line is shown in figure 8.3. The line opened for business is the 31.36 km of double track between Zoo and Jiaochangkou (13 stations, comprised of 10 elevated stations and three underground stations with an average distance between stations of 1 km), which is the first commercial phase of the Jiao-

Xin Line (covering 18 km from Jiaochangkou to Xin shan cun). The minimum radius of curvature of the track is 100 m, maximum gradient is 50%, and the minimum radius of curvature of the train depot is 50 m.

Figure 8.3　Chongqing monorail

Situated in the upper floors of a high-rise block in Daping Station, an integrated government office housing an operations room and other management departments runs the monorail system. Moreover, the platforms of the three underground stations are fitted with screen-type safety doors.

At present, second construction phase of track between Zoo and Xinshancun is under way, and when it is completed, 5.5 km of track with five elevated stations will be added. The assumed passenger volume (one way for the one-hour peak) that can be transported was taken as 12600 people for four-compartment trains in the initial period, 23000 for six-compartment trains the medium term, and 32000 people for eight-compartment trains in the future. The length of the station platforms — which can accommodate trains with up to eight compartment — is 120 m.

8.2.1　Chongqing Monorail Rolling Stock

Rolling stock comprised of 21 trains (making 84 cars) was manufactured. Two prototype trains (8 cars) and the bogies for 10 production trains (40 cars) were manufactured in Japan, and the 19 bodies of production-quality trains (76 cars) and the bogies of nine trains (36 cars) were manufactured at Changchun Railway Vehicles Co., Ltd. under license from Hitachi. Based on the specifications of metropolitan monorails in Japan, the specifications of the Chongqing monorail were defined in consideration of the environmental conditions in Chongqing and Chinese domestic production. The specifications of the rolling stock are listed in table 8.1.

Table 8.1 Main specifications of monorail cars

Items	Specifications
Type	Large-scale straddle-type monorail
Vehicle type	Electric car with double axle bogie truck
Organization	4 car permanently coupled
Passenger capacity	Mc vehicle: 151 persons; M vehicle: 165 persons (Chinese standard)
Electrical system	DC: 1500 V
Track dimensions	Width: 850 mm; height 1500 mm
Loading capacity	Axle load 11t(max.)
Performance	Acceleration: 3.0 km/h/s; Deceleration — Normal: 4.0 km/h/s; Emergency: 4.5 km/h/s
Maximum gradient	60‰ (design value)
Minimum curve radius	50 m (at center between tracks)
Main electrical specification	Three-phase cage-type induction motor (105 kW × 12 units for each train)
Control unit	VVVF traction inverter
Brake unit	Electric-command-type electro-pneumatic straight air brake with regenerative brake
Signal protection	Continuous train detection system and cab-signal automatic train protection
Communication equipment	Train wireless
Operating system	ATP two-manoperated
Low-voltage power source	85-KVA SIV (2 units per train)
Collector	Sliding collection from the side of trolley wire
Ventilation units	Roof-mounted inverter control system(8 units per train)
Emergency exit	"Slow down" handles (1 set per compartment)

Mc: control motor   M: motor   DC: direct current   SIV: static inverter
VVVF: variable voltage, variable frequency   ATP: automatic train protection

(1) Main Car Body

Extruded aluminum is used as the material for the train body, and the roof and sides are composed of a single-skin structure. The exteriors of the aluminumcar bodies are painted to protect against acid rain. As for the acid-rain protection, not only is the coating selected carefully but also the structure right down to the end sections of the coated parts is taken into consideration. Special features of the body interior are FRP (fiber-reinforced plastic) long seats and stanchion poles installed inside the cars. As an air-conditioning system for handling Chongqing's torrid summer heat, two air conditioners (each with a cooling capacity of 19000 kcal) are installed in each car of the monorail train.

(2) **Bogies**

Based on the two-axle bolster-less bogies used for monorails in Japan, a coating specification for countering Chongqing's acid-rain environment is adopted for the bogies. As for the track tires — which are steel-cord rubber ones containing nitrogen — two are fitted per axle. And to allow easy tire changing, the tires are supported on the bogie frame by means of a cantilever system, and puncture-detection devices for measuring tire pressure and auxiliary wheels made of solid rubber are also fitted. Moreover, the running tires and horizontal tires used are products that have been successful in Japan.

8.2.2 Main Specifications of Electrical Equipment

(1) **Main Circuit-control Unit**

Based on the VVVF traction inverter that has been a success in monorail systems in Japan, the control unit is also protected against acid rain. In addition, as the monorail uses rubber tires on its axles, the elastic behavior of the tires and mechanical vibration from the electrical equipment, as well as suppression of their effects on the electrical control systems, have been carefully considered.

Moreover, control systems and vector-control technology — accomplishments that have been amassed from our experience of monorails in Japan — are utilized. And by improving the accuracy of torque control, a more stable torque output has been achieved, even at times of sudden changes in starting resistance such as immediately following start-up (when the largest mechanical vibration is easily generated).

The main features of the VVVF traction inverter are summarized as follows:

① As for the connections to the main electric motors, two motors are connected in parallel with one VVVF traction inverter; three of these inverters are configured as one unit. In case of a control-unit breakdown, to ensure operation of the monorail continues, each of the inverters can be disconnected so as to assure redundancy in the system.

② As for the body of monorail cars — insulated against ground electric potential — to reduce interference of electromagnetic fields (i.e. induction interference) with signaling equipment, a three-level inverter system is applied, and by using a correction value for carrier frequency at low speeds, generation of noise is suppressed.

③ To cut down on maintenance costs, the inverters are fitted with a self-diagnosis inspection function, which allows input parts and control outputs of various sensors to be confirmed, thereby improving the efficiency of inspection.

(2) **Auxiliary-power Unit**

As an auxiliary-power unit, for supplying AC (alternating current) power to the air-conditioners, etc., an 85-KVA static-type converter is used. Three kinds of output power — namely, three-phase 380 V, DC 110 V, and DC 24 V — are supplied according to the different loads on each car.

(3) **Monitor Control Unit**

A monitor control unit, with functions for recording and conditions and operation status of the devices inside the monorail cars, is utilized. This unit is composed of a display panel installed in the driver's cab, a CPU (central-processing unit), and terminals installed in the middle car. The CPU and terminals are connected to the main electrical equipment in the cars by a current-loop transmission system, and they collect car-status record data and event record data from each device. The collected data are then displayed on the panel in the driver's cab. Moreover, the event record data can be sent from the CPU to be read out on a PC of a maintenance engineer in such a way that makes analysis of abnormal events easy.

(4) **ATP/TD Unit**

In the case of this monorail system, an on-board signal stoppage system is adopted. The main features of this system are summarized as follows:

① ATP receiver. As regards the ATP receivers, by means of ATP track-based devices, train position status of an approaching train and track-setting conditions are transmitted to the train as a speed-limitation signal via an induction loop [ATP/TD (train detection) loop] set up continuously along the ground. This signal is continuously received and decoded by antennas fixed to the roof the train. That is, while lighting up on-board signal lights in the cab, it carries speed-limitation and stop information from each ATP control unit.

② TD unit. The TD unit transmits a high-frequency TD signal (indicating the train location) from an antenna on the car roof to the ATP induction loop set up continuously along the ground beside the track.

③ ATP control unit. The ATP control units are train-protection devices that are linked to signaling gear on the ground controlled according to relative distance between one train and the next. While the ATP speed-limitation signal corresponding to the track conditions is displayed in the cab, the train is automatically stopped or is slowed down according to that speed limit, thereby assuring safe train operation. As for the ATP speed checking, train speed detected by a speed generator and the ATP speed-limitation signal received from the track-side ATP units are compared, and in the case that the train speed exceeds the speed limit, an ATP braking command is output, and the train is automatically slowed down.

8.3 Writing: How to Write A Summary

Summarizing means giving a concise overview of a text's main points in your own words. A summary is always much shorter than the original text.

Writing a summary does not involve critiquing or analyzing the source — you should simply provide a clear, objective, accurate account of the most important information and ideas, without copying any text from the original and without missing any of the key points.

(1) Tips for Writing a Good Summary

Whether you're summarizing an event, novel, play, or newspaper article, being able to write an effective one-paragraph summary is an important skill for every writer to possess. For some tips on how to write a good summary, see below:

Find the main idea. A useful summary distills the source material down to its most important point to inform the reader. Pick the major point you want to communicate to the reader, and use your limited sentences wisely to convey it. Take down a few notes to help outline your thoughts in an organized manner.

Keep it brief. A summary is not a rewrite — it's a short summation of the original piece. A summary paragraph is usually around five to eight sentences. Keep it short and to the point. Eliminate redundancies or repetitive text to keep your paragraph clear and concise.

Write without judgment. If you are summarizing an original text or piece of media, you are gathering and condensing its most relevant information, not writing a review. Write your summary in your own words, and avoid adding your opinion.

Make sure it flows. Transitions are incredibly helpful when it comes to building momentum in your writing. Connect your sentences with transition words, making sure they flow together and convey your summary clearly.

(2) Example Summary Writing Format

In the essay Santa Ana, author Joan Didion's main point is (state main point). According to Didion "... passage 1 ..." (para. 3). Didion also writes "... passage 2 ..." (para. 8). Finally, she states "... passage 3 ..." (para. 12) Write a last sentence that "wraps" up your summary; often a simple rephrasing of the main point (figure 8.4).

Example of a concise article summary

> Using national survey data, Davis et al. (2015) tested the assertion that "an apple a day keeps the doctor away" and did not find statistically significant evidence in support of this hypothesis. While people who consumed apples were slightly less likely to use prescription medications, the study was unable to demonstrate a causal relationship between these variables.

Figure 8.4 Example of a concise article summary

8.4 KEY TERMS

(1) monorail
(2) suspended monorail
(3) supported(straddling) monorail
(4) narrow beam
(5) six-car TUs
(6) right of way (ROW)
(7) rubber-tire support
(8) guide ways
(9) movable beam
(10) controversial
(11) mode
(12) TD unit
(13) ATP control unit
(14) track-side

8.5 EXERCISES

Ⅰ Match the terms with correct definitions or explanations.

| monobeam | supported monorail | guideway | suspended monorail |

1. In transit systems, a track or other riding surface (including supporting structure) that supports and physically guides transit vehicles specially designed to travel exclusively on it. (   )

2. In which vehicles straddle the guideway or are laterally supported by it; supported monorails are stabilized by gyro, overhead rails, or lateral guidewheels on both sides of the beam (saddle monorail). (   )

3. A type of guideway that consists of a single beam, usually elevated. It generally has a rectangular cross section that is usually straddled by the associated vehicles. (   )

4. In which vehicles hang directly below the guideway (symmetrical monorail) or to one side of it (asymmetrical monorail). (   )

Ⅱ Answer the following questions according to the text.

1. What is the suspended monorail?

2. What is the supported(straddling) monorail?

3. Compare suspended with supported monorail.

4. State and explain the differences between rubber-tired and rail-guided transit technologies.

Chapter 9　Fully Automatic Operation (FAO)

Driverless operation is a sine qua non for all guided modes with medium-size vehicles serving medium volume lines, since the main purpose of not using large vehicles with lower cost per space is to provide a higher frequency of service. That is possible only if the vehicles/TUs are automated, because manual operation would make their operating costs so high that they would in many cases be rendered economically infeasible.

Physical and operational feasibility of fully automatic operation of transit TUs requires three basic features: first, that vehicles operate on fully protected ROW (category A) to prevent obstacles; second, that they are physically guided (by the guideway); and third, that they have electric propulsion. Specific guidance technology, vehicle size, and other physical features of transit systems have no direct influence on their conduciveness to full automation. Many conventional rail systems — metros and LRRT — now utilize ATO, and an increasing number of new systems are fully automated (i.e., have no crew members).

However, because operation of TUs without crews is more important for intermediate than for high-capacity guided modes, the first driverless operation of a complex transit system (network with many stations and different routings of vehicles) was the Airtrans system, opened in the Dallas — Fort Worth Airport in 1974. The first such system applied to transit service in a city was the Morgantown AGT system, often misnomered as a "PRT", opened in 1975. Subsequently, the number of AGT systems, rubber-tired as well as rail systems, accelerated, so that in 2006 there were over 40 AGT systems in operation. Most of them operate as APMs in airports, but an increasing number also serve transit lines. Several unconventional modes were intended to operate with on-call stopping, i.e., the TUs would only stop when requested by passengers, as is done on many bus and streetcar lines. However, this feature may be used only with small vehicles that operate at very short headways, so that many vehicles would find stations without passenger demand for stopping.

As experience has shown that most AGT and APM systems require rather large TUs (one to three vehicles with 80-space to 100-space capacity), the probability of no passenger calls at some stations becomes very small. Therefore most APM systems at airports and other locations and all fully automated rail systems operate with precisely scheduled stopping plans. Some transit systems have some TUs that do not stop at some stations but on a precisely scheduled and announced basis, such as skip-stop, express trains, zonal service, etc.

9.1 Grades of Fully Automatic Operation

Full-automatic operation system includes automation levels GoA3 and GoA4, that is, the operation mode of full-automatic operation system includes Driverless (manned) automatic operation (DTO) and unattended automatic operation (UTO). Full-automatic operation system is shown in figure 9.1.

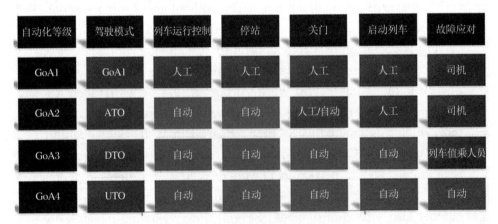

Figure 9.1 Full-automatic operation system

According to the International Association of Public Transport (UITP), there are five Grades of Automation (GoA) for trains: Grades of Automation for trains is shown in table 9.1. Systems (including CBTC) assume responsibility for more functions with increasing GoA is shown in table 9.2.

Table 9.1 Grades of Automation (GoA) for trains

Grade of automation	Train operation	Description
GoA 0	On-sight	No automation
GoA 1	Manual	A train driver controls starting and stopping, operation of doors and handling of emergencies or sudden diversions.
GoA 2	Semi-automatic (STO)	Starting and stopping are automated, but a driver operates the doors, drives the train if needed and handles emergencies. Many ATO systems are GoA 2.
GoA 3	Driverless (DTO)	Starting and stopping are automated, but a train attendant operates the doors and drives the train in case of emergencies.
GoA 4	Unattended train operation (UTO)	Starting and stopping, operation of doors are all fully automated without any on-train staff. It is recommended that stations have platform screen doors installed.

Table 9.2 Compare CBTC with FAO

Basic functions of train operation		On-sight	Non-Automated	Semi-Automated	Driverless	Unattended
		GoA0	GoA1	GoA2	GoA3	GoA4
Ensure safe movement of trains	Ensure safe route	Ops staff (route by systems)	Systems	Systems	Systems	Systems
	Ensure safe separation of trains	Ops staff	Systems	Systems	Systems	Systems
	Ensure safe speed	Ops staff	Ops staff (partial by system)	Systems	Systems	Systems
Drive train	Control acceleration and braking	Ops staff	Ops staff	Systems	Systems	Systems
Supervise guideway	Prevent collision with obstacles	Ops staff	Ops staff	Ops staff	Systems	Systems
	Prevent collision with persons on tracks	Ops staff	Ops staff	Ops staff	Systems	Systems

Continued

Basic functions of train operation		On-sight	Non-Automated	Semi-Automated	Driverless	Unattended
		GoA0	GoA1	GoA2	GoA3	GoA4
Supervise passenger transfer	Control passengers doors	Ops staff	Ops staff	Ops staff	Ops staff	Systems
	Prevent injuries to persons between cars or between platform and train	Ops staff	Ops staff	Ops staff	Ops staff	Systems
	Ensure safe starting conditions	Ops staff	Ops staff	Ops staff	Ops staff	Systems
Operate a train	Put in or take out of operation	Ops staff	Ops staff	Ops staff	Ops staff	Systems
	Supervise the status of the train	Ops staff	Ops staff	Ops staff	Ops staff	Systems
Ensure detection and management of emergency situations	Detect fire/smoke, derailment, loss of train and manage passenger requests (call / evacuation, supervision)	Ops staff	Ops staff	Ops staff	Ops staff	Systems and/or staff in OCC

9.2 Autonomous Train Applications

Advancements in rail technology are quickly taking it to the next level from partial or no automation to a full automation level. Highly sophisticated cutting-edge technologies are being used or planned to be used to achieve the full automation level in trains. A few of these technologies that are used in combination are high-speed internet (5G) technology, infrared cameras, ultrasonic cameras, dedicated short-range communications, accelerometers, tachometers, sensors, among others. Based on the International Association of Public Transport framework, there are four grades of automation (GoAs) for trains that include the following:

GoA1: All the major train operations, such as starting, stopping, door operations, addressing emergency situations, and sudden diversions, are manual and involve an on-board driver.

GoA2: Some of the train operations, such as starting train, stopping, changing the rail tracks, are automated but an onboard driver is still needed.

GoA3: This level provides autonomous train operations, but in case of an emergency an onboard attendant takes control of the train.

GoA4: At this level, the train runs fully autonomous with no onboard driver/attendant (figure 9.2).

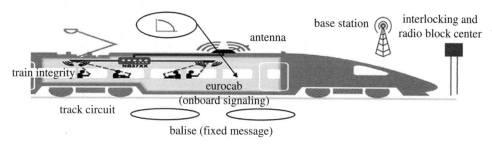

Figure 9.2 An example of a fully autonomous passenger train

Autonomous train features:

The Railway Technical Research Institute (RTRI, Japan) addressed the sustainable development goals by introducing various research activities as a part of the initiative "RESEARCH 2025" and emphasized on the goals of innovation, industry, and infrastructure for railroads. The main RTRI objective is to develop solutions to different challenges facing the railroad industry (e.g. global environmental problems, social burden associated with aging populations, regional disparity of the economy) in cooperation with the railroad practitioners, research institutions, academic institutions, and other relevant stakeholders. The deployment of ATs with the full automation level is one of the strategies to achieve sustainable development goals. Figure 9.3 and figure 9.4 show a variety of innovative technologies that are generally used for operations, movement, and maintenance of ATs. Different technologies are deployed in ATs to provide the information to moving trains regarding the passengers at nearby stations, route control and braking patterns, obstacle detection on the tracks or in the vicinity of tracks, entire line operations, disaster prevention and maintenance information, safety and ground equipment control, and the information regarding the location of neighboring trains. ATs also use onboard data measurement devices, which help in early detection of any abnormalities on tracks and structures. Multiple-point synchronized-control type elastic switches, also known as intelligent switches, are deployed on tracks for detection and collecting some operational data. Various types of data collected assist with the development of big data analysis models for improving the effectiveness of AT operations.

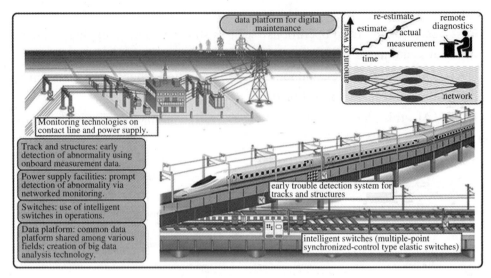

Figure 9.3　Basic AT operations

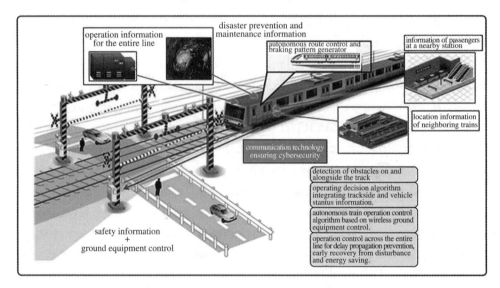

Figure 9.4　Digitalized maintenance for ATs

9.3　Challenges from the Deployment of ATs

As a result of the conducted state-of-the-practice and state-of-the-art review, many different challenges from the AT deployment have been identified and classified into the following categories: ① design challenges; ② operational challenges; ③ technology-related challenges; ④ human aspect-related challenges. The identified challenges are discussed in the following sections.

(1) **Design Challenges**

Although the automation of rail transportation is viewed as less complicated to implement as compared to road transportation, the AT risk management issues do exist.

In particular, the AT operations in emergency situations have to be investigated more in depth. The AT braking distance due to emergency situations has to be optimized (i.e. generally larger weight of trains requires longer stopping distance) to prevent a high impact due to collisions and unforeseeable activities on tracks, such as intrusion by animals or trespassing. Adequate design improvements have to be made to ensure a proper response of ATs in emergency situations.

Along with the automation of trains, the relevant stakeholders should increase the level of automation for maintenance procedures. Some of the critical maintenance procedures that could be fully automated include ballast replacement, ballast tamping, as well as track relaying. Fully automated maintenance procedures are expected to ensure the adequate operational conditions of the rail infrastructure and avoid potential delays of ATs along the rail lines.

One of the advantages from the AT deployment is an increase in the capacity and rail line utilization due to shorter headways between consecutive ATs. Due to shorter headways, the rail terminal designs have to be upgraded to ensure that the train turnaround requirements are met. The future AT terminals should have specific areas designated for train storage (when they are not being deployed), coupling and decoupling of train units, and maintenance procedures.

Another significant challenge that substantially slows down the AT development and deployment is associated with legal issues. The existing laws and regulations put a lot of emphasis on safety and security and require extensive testing of the AT technologies before they could be implemented in practice. Railroad companies, researchers, government representatives, and other relevant stakeholders should collaboratively develop more effective policies that could facilitate the AT development and deployment considering the perspectives of future users and without affecting the safety level.

(2) **Operational Challenges**

ATs are being continuously developed and upgraded in many countries. However, it will not be possible to fully automate all passenger and freight rail lines at the same time (i.e. manually-driven trains will have to share rail lines with ATs, which may create some operational challenges). New policies and operation a strategies should be developed to improve coordination of trains at shared rail lines, so that manually-drive trains can co-exist with ATs.

ATs rely on a wide range of different systems, and the interoperability between these systems should be steadily enhanced. Otherwise, the future ATs will not be able to reach their full potential in the operational effectiveness. One of the approaches the can be used to improve the interoperability of AT systems is the implementation of semantic data models. The semantic data models allow an effective integration of the data generated by various systems.

The future research should investigate different coordination mechanisms between various autonomous systems (e. g. , how to minimize the total waiting time of autonomous buses that expect the arrival of certain passengers that are travelling on an AT). Without effective coordination mechanisms the users of autonomous systems may not be able to experience all the benefits of automation. Furthermore, a lack of effective coordination mechanisms may lead to certain operational deficiencies (e. g. , excessive idle time of autonomous buses and ATs).

Operations scheduling problems generally have high computational complexity, and efficient solution algorithms are required to solve these problems. To ensure a successful AT deployment, many different planning and scheduling problems have to be solved, including train line balancing, timetable development and optimization, real-time train rescheduling, train reordering, and track maintenance. The future studies should concentrate on the development of efficient solution algorithms for these decision problems.

(3) **Technology-related Challenges**

There is a continuous evolution process in rail signaling systems, where communication-based train control systems (e. g. radio technology, microwave technology) are being used instead of track-circuit signaling. Additional steps and procedures have to be undertaken by the relevant stake holders to ensure a smooth transition from one rail signaling system to another.

Despite the fact that the existing ATs rely on a variety of AI-based technologies, more research still has to be done in order to improve the informational, decisional, and learning processes. These processes have to be performed considering a variety of physical and operational attributes, including the train speed and location, speed and location of other trains on a given rail line, presence of objects on tracks, status of railroad signals, and others. Effective informational, decisional, and learning processes will improve the reliability of AT operations.

More efforts should be geared towards improving cyber security of ATs. Cyber-attacks may substantially disrupt the AT operations, as ATs heavily rely on the computer-based AI technologies. Such disruptions may negatively affect the comfort of passengers or even lead to safety issues. Therefore, robust cybersecurity measures should be developed in the future to prevent unauthorized access in the AT computer systems. Moreover, the future ATs should be programmed accordingly, so the required software updates are regularly performed, and the AT computers remain resilient to the new and already-known cyber-threats.

The future research should focus more on enhancing the existing wireless sensor networks, especially in the railroad environments. There exist several issues associated with wireless sensor networks that have to be addressed, including communication reliability, fast transmission rates, measurement of vibrations, management of high-volume data, energy harvesting, energy efficiency, and data fusion.

Throughout the AT operations, there is always a risk of intrusion of people or objects on rail tracks. The existing communication and surveillance technologies have to be enhanced to make sure that unexpected objects on rail tracks will be detected in a timely manner, so ATs could respond properly (e. g. make an emergency stop due to trespassing). This will also help improving safety and security of passengers.

The COVID-19 pandemic made substantial impacts on public transit services around the world and caused a significant reduction in ridership. The future rail transit systems, including autonomous rail transit systems, should have additional protective measures against the spread of airborne diseases (e. g. advanced air circulation, ultraviolet light disinfection). Such measures will help preventing the impacts of airborne diseases on rail transit system operations and improve safety of passengers.

(4) **Human Aspect-related Challenges**

Train drivers perform many different functions (i. e. anticipation, observation, interpretation, and reaction to events). Moreover, train drivers are viewed as a link between different actors involved in various rail operations. There still exists a major challenge in understanding all the roles performed by train drivers and how these roles can be performed by ATs. The safety level and quality of service may drastically decline if ATs are not able to perform the main train driver roles.

User perception remains one of the AT deployment barriers. Based on the conducted review, many users still have concerns regarding the AT performance in emergency situations without the onboard staff. Additional educational programs should be developed and administered, so the future users will be aware of how ATs operate not only under normal but also under disruptive conditions and emergency situations as well. Furthermore, the existing policies should be modified to allow the users accessing autonomous public transportation systems even during the test phases, so they could become more familiar with new technologies and have positive experience in the future.

The existing communication systems within ATs must be improved. The ATs used on metro rail lines should not only be able to communicate with the surrounding infrastructure and other ATs but with the onboard passengers as well. Generally, train drivers inform passengers in case of changes in the planned schedule or emergency situations. Since ATs won't have any onboard staff, the pertinent information should be transmitted by the operational center directly into ATs in the form of the voice messages and/or text messages and/or videos, so the passengers will have the pertinent information throughout their journey.

One of the main concerns with the AT deployment in many countries is associated with the employment issues. Based on the existing projections, the AT deployment can reduce the train crew size by 30%~70% and result in layoffs. Layoffs may further cause a large number of strikes by railroad unions. The employment issues due to the AT deployment have to be addressed by the appropriate stakeholders in the nearest future, as they may substantially slow down the AT development and deployment. The re-orientation of employees (e.g., transition to customer service or to non-automated rail lines) would be a promising solution rather than layoffs or salary cuts.

9.4 Writing: How to Write A Report

(1) What Is A Report?

A report is a document that presents the results of an investigation, project or initiative. It can also be an in-depth analysis of a particular issue or data set. The purpose of a report is to inform, educate and present options and recommendations for future action. Reports are an integral element of dozens of industries, including science, healthcare, criminal justice, business and academia. Reports typically consist of several key elements, including:

Detailed summaries of events or activities.

Analysis of the impact of the event.

Evaluations of the facts and data.

Predictions for what may happen as a result of an event.

Recommendation for next course of action.

(2) Report Writing Format

Here are the main sections of the standard report writing format:

Title Section — This includes the name of the author(s) and the date of report preparation.

Summary — There needs to be a summary of the major points, conclusions, and recommendations. It needs to be short as it is a general overview of the report. Some people will read the summary and only skim the report, so make sure you include all the relevant information. It would be best to write this last so you will include everything, even the points that might be added at the last minute.

Introduction — The first page of the report needs to have an introduction. You will explain the problem and show the reader why the report is being made. You need to give a definition of terms if you did not include these in the title section, and explain how the details of the report are arranged.

Body — This is the main section of the report. There needs to be several sections, with each having a subtitle. Information is usually arranged in order of importance with the most important information coming first.

Conclusion — This is where everything comes together. Keep this section free of jargon as most people will read the Summary and Conclusion.

Recommendations — This is what needs to be done. In plain English, explain your recommendations, putting them in order of priority.

Appendices — This includes information that the experts in the field will read. It has all the technical details that support your conclusions.

Remember that the information needs to be organized logically with the most important information coming first.

Sample Report

Typical structure template for writing a committee report:
Members to which the report is meant for
  [Name, institution, location, Chair]
  [Name, institution, location, member]
  [Date, Time, and Location]
  [Provide simple documentation of any meetings of the committee or subset of the committee, in whatever mode and format, e. g., in person, conference call, etc.]
Purpose
  [Here you mention the purpose of the report in a brief. This enables the reader to understand the purpose behind writing the format.]
Issues
  [Write different issues as sub headings and explain their highlights in bullet points below the respective sub headings]
  • Current Status
  • Accomplishments / Issue 1
  • Future Goals
Near-Term Plans / Main Body of the Report
  [Use Sub Headings as and where needed. In bullet form, outline near-term actions and plans as well under those sub headings.]
Informal Recommendation(s)

[An opportunity to make recommendations, suggestions, and comments to the Board and Executive Director]
Respectfully Submitted
   [Author's Name]

9.5　KEY TERMS

(1) FAO (fully automatic operation)
(2) driverless operation
(3) medium-size vehicle
(4) medium volume
(5) physical and operational feasibility
(6) different routings
(7) transit unit (TUs)
(8) light rail rapid transit (LRRT)
(9) personal rapid transit (PRT)
(10) automated people mover (APM)
(11) skip stop
(12) grades of automation (GoA)
(13) international public transport association (UITP)
(14) autonomous train (AT)
(15) cyber security

9.6　EXERCISES

Ⅰ　Match the terms with correct definitions or explanations.

| unattended train operation (UTO)　　driverless train operation (DTO) |
| automated people mover (APM) |

1. No driver or attendant required on-board the train for normal operation.　(　)

2. A guided transit mode that is fully automated, featuring vehicles that operate on

guideways with exclusive right-of-way. ( )

3. Starting and stopping are automated, but a train attendant operates the doors and drives the train in case of emergencies. ( )

Ⅱ **Answer the following questions according to the text.**

1. What are the differences between GoA1 and GoA4?

2. Describe the present prospects of AFO.

3. Compare FAO system with CBTC system.

References

［1］ 叶清贫，曾毅. 轨道交通运输与信号专业英语[M]. 武汉：华中科技大学出版社，2013.
［2］ 陈兴杰. 城市轨道交通信号专业英语[M]. 北京：中国铁道出版社，2014.
［3］ 李建民. 城市轨道交通专业英语[M]. 北京：机械工业出版社，2010.
［4］ 闵丽平. 城市轨道交通专业英语[M]. 北京：中国铁道出版社，2006.
［5］ 周琪琪，张妮妮，陈冬梅. 城市轨道交通专业英语[M]. 成都：西南交通大学出版社，2015.
［6］ 刘聪慧，贾文婷. 城市轨道交通专业英语[M]. 北京：北京交通大学出版社，2015.
［7］ FAROOQ J，SOLER J. Radio communication for communications-based train control（CBTC）：a tutorial and survey[J]. IEEE Communications Surveys & Tutorials，2017，19(3)：1377-1402.
［8］ YIN J，TANG T，YANG L，et al. Research and development of automatic train operation for railway transportation systems：a survey[J]. Transportation Research Part C Emerging Technologies，2017(85)：548-572.
［9］ 王铸. 城市轨道交通信号技术[M]. 东营：中国石油大学出版社，2015.
［10］ 应婷婷，伍帅英. 轨道交通专业英语[M]. 北京：中国铁道出版社，2015.
［11］ 曹峰. 轨道交通信号专业英语[M]. 北京：中国铁道出版社，2020.
［12］ 林瑜筠，吕永昌. 计算机联锁[M]. 北京：中国铁道出版社，2016.
［13］ 王瑞峰. 铁路信号运营基础[M]. 北京：中国铁道出版社，2014.
［14］ 林瑜筠. 区间信号自动控制[M]. 北京：中国铁道出版社，2017.
［15］ 刘伯鸿. 车站信号自动控制[M]. 北京：中国铁道出版社，2019.
［16］ 郜春海. 基于通信的列车运行控制（CBTC）系统[M]. 北京：中国铁道出版社，2018.
［17］ VUKAN R. Vuchic，urban transit systems and technology[M]. New York：John Wiley & Sons，Inc.，2007.
［18］ VUCHIC，VUKAN R. Urban Transit Operations，Planning and Economics[M]. New York：John Wiley & Sons Inc.，2005.
［19］ SEKITANI T，HIRAISHI M，YAMASAKIS，et al. China's first urban monorail system in Chongqing[J]. Hitachi Review，2005：193-197.
［20］ GRAY B H. Urban Public Transportation Glossary[J]. Urban Transportation，1989，40(1)：23-30.
［21］ SINGH P，DULEBENETS M A，PASHA J，et al. Kampmann，Deployment of Autonomous Trains in Rail Transportation：Current Trends and Existing Challenges[J]. IEEE Access，2021(9)：91427-91461.